Endorsements

" *White Whine* literally saved my life. How, you ask? Well, I recently had a harrowing flying experience. Immediately after takeoff, my flight attendant attempted to give me a business-class blanket—*in my first-class cabin.* 'We're out,' she told me. Wow. There's a difference, obviously. I considered suicide right then and there, but then I remembered what was in my seatback pocket. I grabbed Streeter's book and started reading. The book was okay (I'm not much of a 'reader'), but it was enough to distract me from the disgustingly low thread count making contact with my skin for the remainder of the flight. Thanks, Streeter. "

—**Ricky Van Veen**, founder of CollegeHumor.com

" Streeter is so funny that if he were a wine, he'd be a big glass of MerLOL! Yes, I realize that joke is terrible. But not as terrible as the fact that I have to take the case off my iPhone 5 in order to plug it into the Bose SoundDock I keep by my Jacuzzi. That's bullshit. "

—**Pete Holmes**, comedian

" From the trauma of choosing the wrong line at Whole Foods to the heartbreak that comes with having an overly chatty masseuse, Streeter Seidell delivers a smart and wonderful survey of all the things I haven't been complaining about, but really should be. "

—**Mangesh Hattikudur**, editor of *Mental_Floss* magazine

" Only Streeter could take one of society's most obnoxious habits and make it laugh-out-loud funny with his clever, insightful commentary and uncanny ability to find the best (worst) offenders. I would say I love it, but the font on my book blurb is too small. "

—**Sarah Schneider**, *Saturday Night Live*

Published by
Adams Media, a division of F+W Media, Inc.
57 Littlefield Street, Avon, MA 02322. U.S.A.
www.adamsmedia.com

ISBN 10: 1-4405-5713-6
ISBN 13: 978-1-4405-5713-2
eISBN 10: 1-4405-5714-4
eISBN 13: 978-1-4405-5714-9

Printed in the United States of America.

10 9 8 7 6 5 4 3 2 1

This book is available at quantity discounts for bulk purchases.
For information, please call 1-800-289-0963.

White Whine

=== A STUDY OF ===
FIRST-WORLD PROBLEMS

Streeter Seidell
Creator of WhiteWhine.com

Avon, Massachusetts

Acknowledgments

Hello people who will be reading this part of the book and looking for their name. I hope I didn't forget to include you . . . though, to be honest, I'm deliriously tired so if I forgot to put you in here, forgive me.

Thank you to my wife, Vanessa, for her unending patience and support while I bitched and moaned about writing this book from start to finish. Thank you to my family, new and old, who have always supported me in whatever weird little thing I decide I want to try and who seem to only remember my few triumphs and none of my many failures. Thank you to Charlie Olsen at Inkwell who saw potential in my little website before anyone else. Thank you to Brian Steinberg and Jamie Afifi for handling all of my business affairs so I could focus on being an overgrown child getting paid to write penis jokes. A massive thank you to my editors Brendan O'Neill and Meredith O'Hayre for having the skill and tact to tell me something I've written is terrible in such a way that I didn't realize they were insulting my work. Thanks to Marina Cockenberg for helping spread the gospel of White Whine further than I ever could with her skill, wit, and unabashed spamming. To Ricky Van Veen and Josh Abramson for giving me my start in comedy and letting that start continue for the last nine years. To Anna Hiort and John Zanussi for their help bringing WhiteWhine.com to life and making it look like a legitimate website even though it's something I have exclusively worked on in my underwear. Thank you to all of my friends for their love and support over the years— Keith, Tim, Jeff, Sarah, the Amirs, Kunal, Sam, Amanda, David, Ethan, Kim, Gabrus, Rosie, Jake, Pat, and literally hundreds of others. I have hundreds of friends. It's very important that everybody knows that.

To my mother, father, and sister for giving me a life about which I could not complain. And for my loving wife Vanessa, for listening to me while I complained about it anyway.

Contents

INTRODUCTION...11

57,000 Channels and Nothing On...14
The "News"...16
HD or FU...18
Apple of My Ire...19
The New iPhone...20
The Old Facebook...22
What Do You Mean, No Wi-Fi?...24
My Book Ran Out of Batteries, and Other Modern Complaints...26
GPStress...28
No Service...30
Tumblr—Twitter—Facebook—Is Down!...32
Pinterest Is Down!...34
Phone Groaning...36
Et Tu, Netflix?...38
The Pains of Pandora...40
Too Much Technology...42
Retail Reactions...44
My Name Is Vicki, not Vicky!...46
Consumer Retorts...48
Products, Products Everywhere—And Not a Thing to Buy...50
Money for Nothing...52
Too Rich...54

Checks and Imbalances...56

An Embarrassment by Riches...58

How the Other "Half" "Lives"...60

Whole Foods' Bold Fools...62

The High Cost of Low Class...64

Pining for Poverty...66

Criminal Negligence...68

I Swear, Some People...70

Be Neither Seen Nor Heard...72

No Tip for You...74

Don't You Be My Neighbor...76

Customer Disservice...78

Waiter Haters...80

Yelp, That Was Terrible...82

Bed Dread...84

Bull Sheets...86

Now Lie in It...88

In the Closet...90

The Perils of Single Ply...92

Disappointing Gifts...94

Pet Peeves...96

Under Pressure...98

Harried by Sperry...99

French Cuffs...100

I Don't Wanna Work...102

Music Snobs...104

FestiFAIL...106

Wine Whine...107

The Stars Whine Just Like Us...108

All Hopped Up...110

Um, I Ordered a Complicated Coffee, So 112

CilantrOH NO...114

Vengeful Vegans...116

The Everyday Gourmand...118

Keurig: Changing the Way We Complain about Coffee...120

Trouble in the Water...122

I Ate Too Much...124

Golf Grumbling...125

Training, Complaining at the Gym...126

Nothing Fits My Perfect Body...128

The Stress of Yoga...130

Boat Gloating...132

Going Off the Deep End...134

Horses and Pony Moans...136

White on White: The First-World on Skiing...138

I Need a Vacation from This Vacation...142

Wish You Were Here . . . Instead of Me...144

Paradise Lost...145

The Whitest Whiners...146

Down on the Ground...147

Ugh, Europe...148

Up in the Air...150

First-er Class...152

Hotel Haters...154

Expensive Car, Expansive Whine...156

Beemer Screamers...158

Going Topless...160

Loaner Moaners...162

Charitable Flaws...164

The People vs. the First-World...166
Traffic...168
Never Forget Whine/11...169
White History Month...170
Hyperbole Is Worse Than the Holocaust...172
Foreign Disaster, Local Tragedy...174
Hurricane Pain...176
Shut Up, Mr. President...178
No Habla Anything Other Than This Language...180
Feminisn't...182
Handicapped People: Disabling the Rest of Us...184
The Horror of the Homeless...186
Hipster Bashing...188
Gamer Grief...190
It's My Birthday, and I'll Whine if I Want To...194
Fuck You, Mom and/or Dad...196
Just Die Already!...198
Raising the Next Generation of Whiners...200
I Don't Want to Dye...202
Nail Fail...204
The Problems with Pampering...206
Tan-Trums...208
Tiffany? You're Kidding Me...210
Like Visa, I'm Accepted Everywhere...212
The Doorman...213
No Free Rides on the Scholarship...214
No Place Like Home...216
Luxury^2...219

CONCLUSION...223

Introduction

America was founded on a White Whine. That is, of course, an oversimplification. But there is a reason why the Boston Tea Party has become such an important part of our national creation myth: because we can relate. Oppressive monarchs in faraway lands? Not so much. But paying too much tax on an imported luxury? That strikes a chord with everyone. (Well, at least everyone who bought this book.) From that day on, we have been a proud nation of complainers. And before we get into the thick of it, let's take a little detour to visit the elephant in the room.

Why "White" Whine? My reason is twofold. First of all, I am a comedy writer. And like any comedy writer, I love a good pun (and even enjoy bad ones, which the chapter titles in this book display). When I discovered that the WhiteWhine.com domain name had not been purchased, I snapped it up faster than you could say, "Wow, GoDaddy.com is an ugly, terrible website." Comedy writers cannot and will not abandon a good pun for anything or anyone. So, I'm sticking with it. My second reason is a little more complicated, mostly because it doesn't quite make sense.

As oh-so-many Internet commenters on the website have pointed out, the "white" in "WhiteWhine" doesn't seem to have anything to do with race, which is true. They have also pointed out that I look like a "fat, shaved bear" and a "nose that grew a body," but that is neither here nor there. White is my succinct way to encapsulate a group of people—of any race, mind you—who are financially and domestically comfortable, entitled, and, most importantly, unsatisfied. They are people who have it good but want it better. They have the world in the palm of their hand but complain about how much it weighs. They stop and smell the neighbor's roses and wonder why their own don't smell as good (and then fire their gardener). They are White, whether they are white or not.

See? Doesn't make that much sense. But what was I supposed to do, abandon a solid pun? Please. If my liberal use (and flimsy defense) of this politically incorrect term angers you, I beg you to harness that anger and redirect it. Away from me, and at a much more worthy target: White people.

White like how I explained it above, obviously. Not white white.

You get it.

But, Why Do We Need This Book? It's very simple, really. When our society collapses, as the big ones tend to do from time to time, how will our descendants—postapocalyptic savages that they will be—know how good things once were, if not for this book? Sure, they may dig up an encyclopedia and read of the many wonders of our time. But nothing can quite drive home just how nice of a world we've created for ourselves than to find evidence that, amidst all of those wonders and conveniences, we still found things to bitch about. In fact, more often than not it was the conveniences that were bothering us! So why this book, you ask? To give the remnants of our crumbled society something to strive toward. To inspire some poor man a thousand years from now, clothed in rags, to say, "One day, my descendants will live in a world where they can complain that their Starbucks coffee is too hot! Whatever Starbucks coffee is!"

So What Is a White Whine? There are infinite shades of gray when it comes to classifying the various types of White Whine, but at their core they're just First-World Problems. That is, the notion that no matter how good you have it—drinking coconut water, eating at fancy restaurants, having an iPhone, being able to afford child care—you're still annoyed. That is the common denominator in all White Whines. Allow me to highlight this concept further with an incredibly intricate and beautiful chart.

WHINE	WHITE WHINE
"It's so cold in my apartment."	"It's so cold in my family's ski house."
"Ugh, I'm sick again."	"Ugh, every time I go to Paris I get sick."
"Oh no, I spilled ketchup on my pants!"	"Oh no, I spilled organic ketchup on my J-Crew slim-fit chinos!"

The difference is subtle, but it's there. To be a White Whiner your complaint must convey, simultaneously, that you are both fortunate and irritated.

And with that basic introduction to the world of rich bitching, let me welcome everyone to *White Whine*, the book. I hope you enjoy the fruits of your temper.

57,000 *Channels* and Nothing On

When it comes to TV, people are spoiled for choice. Or they're just spoiled. By my count, there are currently 28,000 cable channels, showing 18 million shows, 2 million movies on demand, and 39 billion terrible documentaries about the dangers of oil/plastic/fishing/lumber/sleeping/drinking milk/and watching too much TV. If people take their digital leisure time even the least bit seriously, they could be watching almost anything that has ever been filmed. Right now. The fact that people are doing anything else other than watching TV—like reading this book, say—only highlights a serious First-World Problem: There's nothing to watch. Except everything.

What's impressive is that even though people can watch basically anything they want, whenever they want it, they still find ways to complain about it. The tens of thousands of free movies on Netflix "all suck," downloading a full season of a show on iTunes "takes forever," and Time Warner digital cable

"Shits out halfway through every movie I try to watch." (That last one is true. Make sure you check your bill, because they'll charge you full price for half a movie, the bastards.)

Perhaps the White Whiniest of all TV complaints come from the lucky few who actually have found a show they want to watch. While you'd think they'd be happy about this incredible achievement, alas, they are not. Why? Because it's going to take forever. "I wanted to watch *The Wire*, but it's like fifty episodes! It will take me a year to watch the whole thing!" This is an entirely new, distinctly First-World Problem: My leisure activity takes too much effort. We have built a society so thoroughly entertained that it actually takes ambition and commitment to be lazy. I think this is something to be proud of; but whiney TV viewers would beg to differ.

I wish time travel existed so I could round up these people and send them back to 1958. Let them enjoy three fuzzy black-and-white channels that air nothing but bad, formulaic sitcoms. Let them try to "get into" a show where the protagonist abruptly stops acting midscene, turns to the camera, and suggests that if you're a pregnant or nursing mother, Chesterfield may be the best cigarettes for you and your baby. Then they'd understand how good they have it. Not only is their modern television so good it takes time and effort to enjoy, but medical science has come a long way as well. These days, everyone knows that pregnant and nursing mothers choose Camel Lights to help their kids grow up strong.

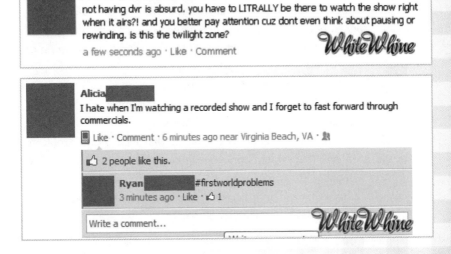

not having dvr is absurd. you have to LITRALLY be there to watch the show right when it airs?! and you better pay attention cuz dont even think about pausing or rewinding. is this the twilight zone?
a few seconds ago · Like · Comment

White Whine

Alicia
I hate when I'm watching a recorded show and I forget to fast forward through commercials.
Like · Comment · 6 minutes ago near Virginia Beach, VA ·

2 people like this.

Ryan #firstworldproblems
3 minutes ago · Like · 1

Write a comment...

White Whine

The *"News"*

The news is how we stay informed about horrible crimes in our neighborhoods, horrible crimes in our schools, horrible scams perpetrated on innocent consumers, horrible products you might not even know are bad for you, and what an adorable kitten did to save her owners. You've got to see it to believe it. All that, and sports with Chris Tanken after the break. As I mentioned, the news usually concerns itself with death, destruction, pain, panic, crime, and misery. But every now and then there is a lull in rapes/murders/fires/wars/diseases, and so the news is forced to cover what they refer to as "puff pieces"—and what everyone else refers to as "bullshit." And in this bullshit grow some of the finest White Whines the news has to offer. Kind of like shrooms.

Sometimes the Whines are intentional. The news knows how ridiculous the puff piece story is. But then again, hey, doesn't everyone like a little laughter mixed in with their stories about kidnapped little kids and the new strain of superflu making its way across Asia? But sometimes the purveyors of puff seem to be blissfully unaware that they're reporting something ludicrous: as if a story about how Subway's footlong subs may actually sometimes be shorter than a full foot is actual news that the world needs to know.

Nowhere does the news's tendency to pretend that First-World Problems are actual problems than when stories are juxtaposed on a screen, ticker, or website. What should get top billing: A deadly natural disaster or how a mishap with a horse marred an otherwise perfect celebrity wedding? I think we know which one is going to win that battle.

In many ways this phenomenon is our fault. We demanded more news, from the TV, from the Internet, even from the newspapers. As our desire for gossip has risen, so have the noble ideals of journalism fallen. We are creating a world that is devoid of substance, a world that instead runs on . . . sorry, we're just getting word now that tea maker Twinings has changed the recipe of its Earl Grey tea, and tea drinkers are not pleased. We'll take you to the Twinings plant now, where reporter Chuck Tarkington has the story.

We're pining for our old Twinings: Furious Earl Grey drinkers dismiss new recipe as 'an affront to tea'

By ALAN WATKINS

Last updated at 8:08 AM on 29th August 2011

💬 Comments (179)| ⬛ Add to My Stories | ⬛ Share

🄵 Like 598

Prince William of Wales »   ☆ ▾

Fallen Horse Is Only Stumble in Carefully Scripted Wedding Day

ABC News - Russell Goldman - 41 minutes ago

A horse falls during the royal wedding parade in London, England on April 29, 2011. ABC News The picture-perfect wedding of Prince William to Kate Middleton today in London went off without a hitch -- almost.

➕ Video: Royal Wedding Raw Video: Royal Fans Celebrate ▶

The Associated Press

USA TODAY's royal wedding photo albums USA Today

Reuters - Daily Mail - Christian Science Monitor - BBC News - Wikipedia: Wedding of Prince William, Duke of Cambridge, and Catherine Middleton

all 21,431 news articles »

CBC.ca

Tornado »   ☆ ▾

Dozens of tornadoes kill at least 297 people in South

USA Today - Marty Roney, Carolyn Pesce - 1 hour ago

TUSCALOOSA, Ala. - The tornadoes roared into cities like runaway freight trains, devouring houses, leveling entire neighborhoods and burying people who scrambled to get away under mounds of dirt and rubble.

➕ Video: Alabama Tornado: Dramatic amateur videos, massive storm aftermath ▶ RT

Tornado death toll expected to rise as searches continue amid devastation Los Angeles Times

New York Magazine - Cleveland Leader - CNN International - al.com (blog)

all 8,310 news articles »

Los Angeles...

HD or FU

The first time I ever saw HDTV I'll admit that I did not like it. It felt too crisp, too sharp. The soft edges that allow a great film to transport you to another world for two hours were gone, replaced by the harsh lines of reality. And so I flipped back to a non-HD channel and found myself suddenly disgusted by the grainy picture, horrible resolution, and muted colors. I was a changed man. Many of us have converted to HD, though some are more committed than others. These devotees cannot go back now, and when they're forced to, their anger is as clear as the beads of sweat forming on Al Roker's forehead. I mean, can you imagine, the indignity of having to watch Al Roker sweat in normal definition?!

Now that they've had the best, they don't want (and won't accept) anything less. To draw a few parallels: they've now gone skiing out west. They've flown First Class. They've driven a Maserati. They've mainlined heroin, and one thing is for damn sure: they're not going back to smoking pot.

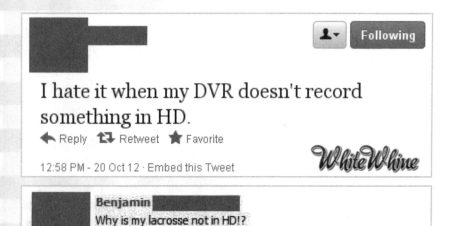

Following

I hate it when my DVR doesn't record something in HD.

← Reply ⇄ Retweet ★ Favorite

12:58 PM - 20 Oct 12 · Embed this Tweet

White Whine

Benjamin

Why is my lacrosse not in HD!?

📱 2 hours ago via Text Message · Like · Comment *White Whine*

18

Apple *of My Ire*

An apple a day may keep the doctor away, but an Apple a day will leave you poorer than Richard (that one is for my high school history teacher). In this extremely clever little maxim, I refer, of course, to Apple computers and their notoriously high price point. But that's not the only thing Apple users complain about. They'll complain about almost everything Apple does while buying almost anything Apple puts out. Apple, along with Starbucks, is one of those companies that people simultaneously deeply love and passionately hate.

Apple fans will wait in lines for days just for the thrill of being the first to complain about their new iPad. They'll type long-winded, scathing critiques of the company's strategy and products from their brand new, $2,199 MacBook Airs. They'll even point out when other companies are doing better, but will still refuse to switch brands. Why? Because Apple puts out the best products on the market right now, so jumping ship would be idiotic. So White Whiney Apple fans will do what they've always done: complain about the company they love with all their heart.

Entire old growth forests would have to die to print all of the Apple White Whines sent to the site in this book, so let's give the trees a break and let this one speak for all of them.

Here's a First World Problem for ya - I've been playing with my new iPad mini and I love it so much that now my iPhone seems tiny and unimpressive. Le sigh.

Like · Comment · 44 minutes ago via mobile ·

👍 2 people like this.

The New iPhone

The iPhone is one of the most important products to hit the shelves in the last decade. Seemingly overnight, the smartphone market was playing by new rules. It was no longer enough to have a phone that made calls and took pictures, it also had to play music, browse the Internet, and have apps. Oh so many apps. And people love their iPhones—deeply—regardless of the iPhone having a price point many hundreds of dollars above its closest competitor. There's really only one problem with the iPhone: the new iPhone. When a new iPhone comes out, Apple fans everywhere begin a Gollum/Sméagol-like internal argument.

"We needs it. We needs the new iPhoneses."

"No. No. No. Our old iPhone is fineses. It playses music and takeses pictures. We loves the old iPhone."

"Tricksy Apple made the new iPhoneses better. We needs the precious. We must have the precious."

Whether they buy a new iPhone or decide to stick with their old iPhone, a torrent of White Whines is the result. For those who bought the new phone, the first order of business is to start complaining about it. Why is the headphone jack upside down? Why is it so big? Why is it so light? Why doesn't it "feel" right in my hand? For people who spent a good amount of time and money just to get this phone, they sure don't seem to like it very much.

But then there is an even sadder group of White Whiners: those who didn't get the new iPhone. Their tweets and statuses read like the diary entries of a grounded rich kid. Why do all of their friends get to have the new $700 thing and they don't? What did they do to deserve this?! Does nobody love them? Their old iPhone, so recently their most cherished possession, is now an embarrassing piece of shit that they're being forced to carry around.

The good news for people deprived of the new iPhone is that soon, within weeks it seems, they will have another chance to give Apple $700 when an even newer iPhone comes out.

…ıl. Verizon 📶   **9:07 PM**   ⏱ 63% 🔋

Home   **Tweet**   ✒

@

i wish i didn't have a shitty 3G iphone because the camera sucks and the sky looks so cool right now and i just wanna instagram it.

1 hour ago

WhiteWhine

The 5 is too big for my hand. The weight is throwing me off too since its awkwardly light.... This phone is made for a mans hand....

Like · Comment · 31 minutes ago via mobile ·

WhiteWhine

21

The Old *Facebook*

Facebook is possibly the greatest communication tool ever created. And good thing, too, because when Mark Zuckerberg decides to change Facebook even slightly, millions of people are able to complain about this latest affront to decency instantly—to hundreds of millions of people. A new design or new feature immediately turns a fair portion of Facebook's users into a pack of pickled old bar drunks who nurse warm pilsners while angrily shouting about the good ol' days to nobody in particular. Their rallying cry of "Bring back the old Facebook!" rings out from page to page, but these calls to action have resulted in an impressive zero rollbacks of code, features, or design.

Brave dissidents unite behind groups with names like "1 million strong to bring back the old Facebook" (238 members), but these revolutionaries have yet to figure out how to take their protests to the next level. That level, of course, would be "actually doing something." Sometimes people will protest by posting, "Like this status to bring the old Facebook back!" which is like saying, "Shop at Walmart to protest Walmart's hiring practices!" The only thing disgruntled Facebook users can do is close their account. And while these threats are often heard, they are rarely carried out. I imagine that somewhere in Quebec the only person to leave Facebook after a redesign is poking at a cold plate of poutine with the only person to move out of America when George W. Bush was re-elected. Just two lonely, principled souls who thought a lot more people would share their same dedication to making good on a threat.

Nostalgia, which produces only rosy visions of the past, should be a Schedule I controlled substance. Think of the conservatives who practically bring themselves to orgasm when they think of America in the 1950s while completely ignoring historic realities such as segregation, the constant threat of nuclear war, and the lack of central air conditioning. While it usually takes a lifetime to erase the painful realities of the past (to the point anyone would actually want to relive it), a proponent for the old Facebook can mentally wipe away any shortcomings of the old design faster than a sorority girl can untag herself in an unflattering picture.

Perhaps Facebook should bring back the old version of the site just for a day. The really old one, the one I eagerly signed up for when my college was finally able to make accounts. Let Facebook's whiniest critics enjoy having one tiny profile photo, no messaging feature, and an active university e-mail account in order to login. The best part? They wouldn't even be able to complain about it because status updates hadn't been invented yet. Cries of "Bring back the old Facebook" would never be heard again, which would allow users to get back to the important business of complaining about everything else.

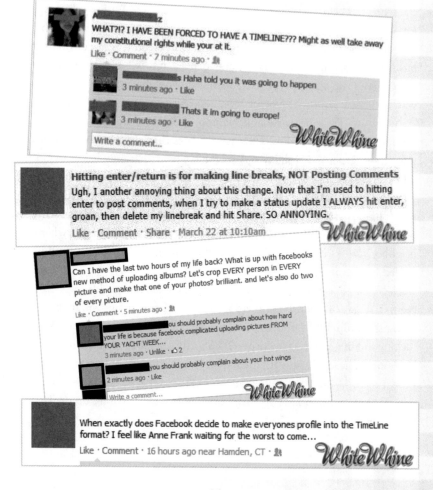

23

What Do You Mean, No Wi-Fi?

"What's the Wi-Fi here?" is probably one of the most asked questions today, right behind, "Do you have any gluten-free options?" Wi-Fi—which stands for Wireless Fi—is no longer seen as a luxury or even a convenience, but as a right. An unalienable, unpassword-protectable right. It is in our homes and businesses, on our busses, trains, and planes, and we use it for important things like keeping track of bills, working remotely, and trying to illegally watch the new season of *Doctor Who* before it premieres in America.

When Wi-Fi is not available, laptop and tablet owners liken it to a trampling of their freedoms. Their pained cries ring out from every corner of the nation. From the Holiday Inn off the highway that only has Wi-Fi in the lobby. From the coffee shop that requires you to be a customer before they give you the password. From the airplane that hasn't been retrofitted with a router yet. From a parents' house where a dial-up modem still beeps and wheezes behind a 1995 Gateway desktop computer. From a new apartment where the neighbor's Wi-Fi is plentiful but fortified by an un-guessable password like a walled Medieval city.

When Wi-Fi is denied in these situations people very quickly pass through the five stages of grief. First, there is denial. "Maybe if I go sit at that table with my laptop, I'll be able to pick up a signal!" Then comes anger. "Are you fucking kidding me, Logan Airport?!" Shortly after, our victim will enter the bargaining phase. "I know it's for staff only, but what if I buy something? Can I use it then?" When bargaining fails to work—as it always does—depression sets in. "I'm going to have to spend my whole night catching up on Tumblr when I get home now . . ."

And finally, only after every option has been exhausted, these victims enter the final stage of grief: acceptance. "I can't believe it's come to this," they sadly mumble as they take out their iPhones and tweet about how the Business Class lounge at Logan Airport doesn't have free Wi-Fi and how that "str8 up suxdonkee dix." Sadly, it could take hours for this insight to reach their follower's eyes. After all, everyone knows the 3G Internet on an iPhone is "slow as shiz."

Dear Carnival Cruise lines: seriously, no WiFi? We are not on speaking terms.

June 25, 2011 10:30:42 AM from Twitter for iPhone

This church doesn't have wi-fi.
#BULLSHIT #CHURCHTWEETS

19 Nov via Twittelator · ☆ Favorite · ↻ Retweet · ↩ Reply

Stays at a hotel in Tokyo. Hotel only has hardwired Internet connection. Has only an iPad. There is something wrong with this picture. And really? What prominent hotel in JAPAN doesn't have wifi?

Like · Comment · Share · 9 hours ago via mobile · 🐜

My Book Ran Out of Batteries, and Other Modern Complaints

"My book ran out of batteries." In six short words this White Whine confirms what we have long suspected: We're currently living in the future. It's strange to believe, but it's true. Our books run on batteries now. And just like most of our appliances—refrigerators, TVs, even cars—they are now smarter than we are. Hell, we even fight wars now by sending out flying robots to kill our enemies, no matter what stands in the way. In other words, we have Terminators.

So, our books run out of batteries. It's the first White Whine of the next generation, and one that confirms what we have long feared: Living in the future is still going to be kind of a pain in the ass. This is nothing new, of course. I'm sure a day or two after we harnessed fire, some idiot caveman was all, "You know, before we did this fire thing I had fingertips, hair, and eyebrows." Progress always presents new problems, and with each advance we will be standing by ready and willing to moan. Yes, we'll be the first to complain about the hover car dynamo rotor being too bright. We'll be the first to moan about how flying Astro Class to the Lunar SpaceDock isn't really worth the price. And we'll be the first to whine about how, just when we finally caved and bought the iSexRobot 3.1, they go ahead and announce that the iSexRobot 3.2 will be out in three months. And the new model has a front-facing camera, too! The front-facing camera is a game changer!

Here it is, folks, the first glimpse at a future full of amazing wonders that we'll almost certainly find really, really irritating.

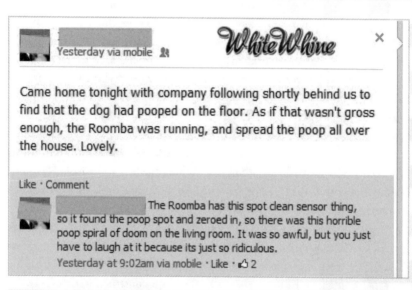

Came home tonight with company following shortly behind us to find that the dog had pooped on the floor. As if that wasn't gross enough, the Roomba was running, and spread the poop all over the house. Lovely.

Like · Comment

The Roomba has this spot clean sensor thing, so it found the poop spot and zeroed in, so there was this horrible poop spiral of doom on the living room. It was so awful, but you just have to laugh at it because its just so ridiculous.
Yesterday at 9:02am via mobile · Like · 👍 2

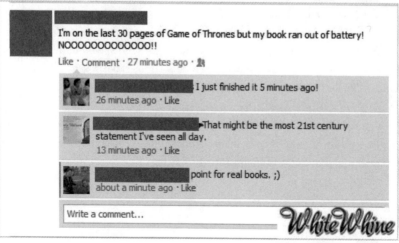

I'm on the last 30 pages of Game of Thrones but my book ran out of battery! NOOOOOOOOOOOOOO!!

Like · Comment · 27 minutes ago ·

I just finished it 5 minutes ago!
26 minutes ago · Like

That might be the most 21st century statement I've seen all day.
13 minutes ago · Like

point for real books. ;)
about a minute ago · Like

Write a comment...

GP Stress

As I just mentioned, we're living in the future. Our old, worn out organic bones are replaced by shiny titanium ones and robots do everything from clean our floors to build our cars. We no longer need to know how to get from point A to point B thanks to a network of satellites and computers, collectively known as GPS. We use GPS to figure out where to drive our hybrid cars, where to ride our fixie bikes, and how close we are to that new vegan muffin store. You know, the one on Smith Street. The one run by the lesbian couple. No, the other lesbian couple.

Most of us are truly lost without our GPS (pardon the pun). But just as GPS answers First-World questions like "What's the best route from Newport, Rhode Island, to Cape Cod," it can cause First-World Problems when it's not working.

At the root of most GPS White Whines is the fact that GPS is a computer system and not a human servant. So while GPS can figure out the shortest distance between two places, and even account for speed limit and traffic patterns, it might not know when, say, there are construction or deadly car accident delays. In other words, GPS doesn't have a set of eyeballs and a brain to analyze the road ahead. I mean, it has a lady's voice, right? Shouldn't it make rational decisions and tell me where to go? And speaking of that voice, why is she so annoying? I mean, can't this robot have a soothing, learned voice? Oh, and while we're at it, how come this idiot robot doesn't know how to pronounce all the local street names like I do?

I'm starting to think that the Garmin suction-cupped to my windshield might not be a sentient, brilliant cyborg but is instead a semipowerful navigational computer I bought for $125 at Best Buy.

Really wish BMWs had an "avoid ghettos" option on there navigation systems

Like · Comment · about an hour ago near Passaic, NJ · 🔒

👍 2 people like this.

Laura [   ] whitewhine.com
about an hour ago · Like

S▮▮arose [   ] Mercedes can kindly follow suit!   ✕
49 minutes ago · Like

Write a comment...   *WhiteWhine*

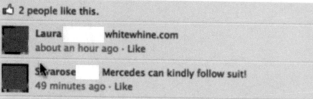

Well. If the blue dot was accurate we would be drowning. Stupid gps

Like · Comment · Share · 4 minutes ago · 🔒   *WhiteWhine*

A[   ]
Seriously? in dash Navigation was unavailable on a rental so I had to use my phone? WTF?

9 hours ago · Like · Comment

P[   ] How have you been? I have not heard from you in ages. Hope things are going well for you...
4 hours ago · Like

M[   ] whitewhine.com
a few seconds ago · Like

Write a comment...   *WhiteWhine*

No Service

If there is one part of our modern world that still confounds me it's cell phones. The Internet I understand. Even Roombas make sense. But I have absolutely no idea how it is even possible to pick up a little piece of plastic, push a few buttons, and talk to someone on the other side of the world . . . in real time . . . without any wires. Each call really does feel like I'm doing a magic trick, even if all I'm doing is calling someone in India to help me change the credit card number on my GrubHub.com account. But cellular magic doesn't come easily to every conjurer—thanks to the fact that no charmed incantation, no devilish spell, no stinking potion, can give a cell phone perfect service everywhere.

If not having access to Wi-Fi is the king of connectivity complaints for White Whiners, then not having cell phone service—or not having the right kind of cell phone service—is the prince. White Whiners in search of service find themselves in precarious situations—often wandering around, cell phone held aloft—searching endlessly for just a few seconds of 3G or 4G. They are like old men walking the beach with metal detectors, hoping to locate some buried LTE frequency out in the middle of nowhere.

The good news is that these White Whiners will always find the service they so deeply desire. How do we know? Because as soon as a connection can be made, they hit Twitter and Facebook to tell the harrowing tale of the Time They Only Had One Bar Of Edge.

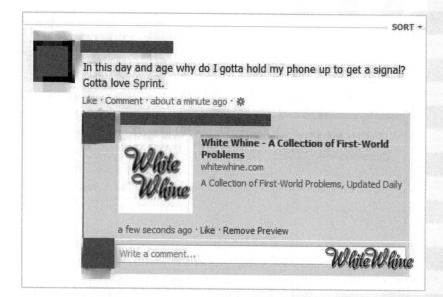

In this day and age why do I gotta hold my phone up to get a signal? Gotta love Sprint.

Like · Comment · about a minute ago · ✳

White Whine - A Collection of First-World Problems
whitewhine.com

A Collection of First-World Problems, Updated Daily

a few seconds ago · Like · Remove Preview

Write a comment...

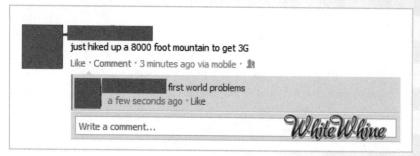

just hiked up a 8000 foot mountain to get 3G

Like · Comment · 3 minutes ago via mobile · 👥

first world problems
a few seconds ago · Like

Write a comment...

Tumblr—Twitter—Facebook—*Is Down!*

One thing you can count on when using a website is that at some point, hopefully not too often, that site just won't work. The causes of "downtime" or "outages" are complicated and varied, but according to White Whiney web users, most outages can be traced back to the fact that "this website is fucking garbage and it sucks all the dicks." The three sites that seem to crash the most, or are at least the most whined about, are Facebook, Twitter, and Tumblr (the "Big 3" as only I call them). Since using any of these sites is the digital equivalent to smoking a big ol' bag of crack, users tend to get a little touchy when they can't get their fix. I completely understand why, too. How will everyone know what I think about the new season of *Girls* if I can't get on Tumblr? How will people know that I'm just chillin' at home with a bottle of wine after a loooooonnnnng week if I can't update my Facebook status? For God's sake, how will I tell my 623 spambot Twitter followers that I serizly H8 drama?! Most important, how will I let everyone know that Twitter is down when Twitter is down? Luckily, all three never seem to go down at the same time. Like digital Paul Reveres, brave heralds ride from website to website warning all who will listen about the terrible tragedy that's befallen our beloved Tumblr or Facebook or Twitter. "Hear ye! Here ye! Twitter is down!" they scream on Facebook to an eager crowd of nobody.

Sometimes I imagine what would happen if all three sites were to go down at once. I imagine one of these White Whiners trying to get to Facebook, only to discover that it is down. So they decide to go to Twitter to tweet about how Facebook is down, only to discover that Twitter is overloaded. And then they get excited because, really, when are the big two both down at the same time? That would make a great Tumblr post! So off they stroll to Tumblr, only to find that Tumblr, too, has gone dark. Left with no other options, I imagine that this netizen would walk to a window, open it as wide as possible, and scream to the heavens about how all three big social networks are down at once. And while they're hanging out the window maybe a slight breeze will kiss their cheek. Maybe a ray of sunshine will caress their hands. Maybe they'll hear the distant laughter of children at a park or the bark of a happy dog. Maybe they'll see the verdant trees and the earthen rock and the blue water and all the beauty that nature so effortlessly paints on the canvas of reality. And then they'll be extra sad because that, too, would make a great Tumblr post.

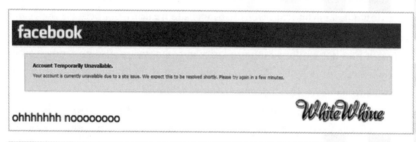

facebook

Account Temporarily Unavailable.
Your account is currently unavailable due to a site issue. We expect this to be resolved shortly. Please try again in a few minutes.

ohhhhhhh nooooooooo

WhiteWhine

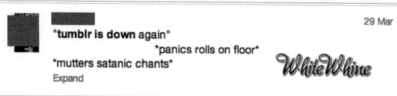

29 Mar

"tumblr is down again"

panics rolls on floor

mutters satanic chants

Expand

WhiteWhine

@maraudercracker   1m

why is tumblr down how am I supposed to live like this

Expand

@itsmemoriahhh   1m

"@Annanicholle - so tumblr is down, there goes my life. sadness. :(" - - THIS! :"(

Expand

:(@fartpalace   1m

lots of people wanna kill themselves because tumblr is down

Expand

© @alinadorothea   1m

tumblr is down i want to cry   *WhiteWhine*

Expand

Pinterest *Is Down!*

We've already discussed what happens when Twitter, Tumblr, or Facebook goes down. Users run from website to website freaking out because they can't post their vacation pictures now?! But Pinterest, the female-focused social network that has exploded in popularity in recent years, also goes down from time to time. And when Pinterest goes down, something entirely different happens to its users: they become helpless White Whiners.

Without their trusty pins, they're no longer able to go grocery shopping since they can't see what kind of interesting produce is being pinned by their friends and family. They can't get dressed since they can't see what the new, cool way to wear a circle scarf is. They can't even plan their wedding since, according to my wife, all of the decorations, the dress, and the party favors are found via Pinterest posts. There are, of course, hundreds of thousands of other websites that could solve all of their problems, but none of those other websites have that fun little pin thing, so they're basically worthless.

For millions of women who use the site for everything from gift ideas to SFW masturbation fodder in the form of pictures of shirtless firemen holding babies, Pinterest crashing is like slamming the brakes on life. No decisions can be made until the wisdom of the pins has been restored. Then, and only then, can these women finally see if any crocheted tea cozies are on Etsy for $20.

And then they can masturbate to that fireman picture, too. All is well in the world.

Chelsea

Oh my gosh I'm at the grocery store and my Pinterest account won't open!!! HOW DO I KNOW WHAT TO BUY FOR MY STEW!!!!!

End of the freaking world!!

Like · Comment · about a minute ago near Granbury, TX · 🔏

👍 2 people like this.

| Write a comment... |

WhiteWhine

---

anti-pinterest

by ██████████ on Wednesday, December 14, 2011 at 4:44pm · 🔏

ok so clearly i'm have a lack-luster day. but i love pinterest. i love getting new ideas for things to craft, cook, wear, and do. but GOOD GOD ALMIGHTY do i get sick of seeing nothing but wedding posts, posts about exercise, and dumb ass posts about "things to do before you die." essentially (as has already been established) i hate humans. i want to tear down all of their pretentious crap that makes them feel better even if it's fake, stupid, or impossible. now after reading that sentence again i realize that i am probably a horrible person. but right now i couldn't care less. i get so IRRITATED with people's simplistic an unoriginal opinions that it just makes me want to scream. SO. the question of the day becomes, how do i block stupid shit from my pinterest, or does anyone know of a similar website with less garbage on it?

thanks to all for tolerating my snarkiness

Like · Comment · Share

R████████V ironic you're posting this on facebook
December 14, 2011 at 5:02pm · Like

M████████ i way to prove her point, dude
December 14, 2011 at 5:14pm · Like

R████████V that's just your simplistic, unoriginal opinion ;)
December 14, 2011 at 5:24pm · Like

S████████w I thoroughly enjoyed this rant.
December 22, 2011 at 4:44pm · Like

| Write a comment... |

WhiteWhine

Phone *Groaning*

There is a base measure of prosperity among urban, upwardly mobile First-Worlders. In the past that might have been a cool car or a boss stereo, but these days it's an iPhone. Having an iPhone says to all the other people at the vegan pastry shop, "I have the latest and greatest in mobile technology and the money to pay for it." It's the ultimate status symbol, and like any status symbol, it's not available to everyone. Alas, some people have been left out of the iPhone bonanza and have to settle for other phones. And they're not happy about it.

Like a high school senior not invited to the cool after-prom party (Which I totally went to. Definitely.), these poor White Whiners are a sad, sorry bunch who cannot take part in the good times all the iPhone owners are having. They're like the one guy at work who decided not to go in on the office lotto pool and now has to watch as all his former coworkers drive away in brand new Bentleys. They're surrounded by iPhones while they're stuck tapping away on an HTC or a Blackberry or an Android.

But don't feel too bad for them. Even though they don't know it, they're the lucky ones. They're not slaves to the new iPhone cycle of desire. They're not locked into Apple's proprietary software. They're not beholden to iTunes's terms of service. So, good for them for being independent and going their own direction. Even if that direction leads to a mountain of White Whines about how they wish they had iPhones.

i just found out im the only one at my lunch table without an iPhone........... high school sucks :(

Like · Comment · 31 minutes ago via Mobile · 👥

👍 3 people like this.

Ta

im trying really hard not to care that everyone around me has an i phone. not only is cheezus getting one, but today i saw an old, obese, white trash couple with 4 teeth between them playing angry birds on sparkling iphone 4s's (with leopard and camouflage phone cases) at crema cafe.
my image is on the rocks, drowning in shame at my lack of whole hearted consumerism. throw me a bone US Cellular.

Like · Comment · 12 minutes ago · 👥

So I've got to send my htc back for repair, this is a disaster! Back to the shatberry for my evenings internet browsing just doesn't cut it!

Like · Comment · 26 minutes ago via Mobile · ☀

> Clearly your in need of a craptop instead
> 25 minutes ago via mobile · Like

> True dat
> 24 minutes ago via mobile · Like

> HTC's are shit!! I have one and its been repaired twice.
> 15 minutes ago via mobile · Like

> www.whitewhine.com
>
> **White Whine - A Collection of First-World Problems**
> whitewhine.com
> A Collection of First-World Problems, Updated Daily
>
> A few seconds ago · Edited · Like · Remove Preview

---

k   23h

If my parents fucking get me the android for christmas I will throw it in their face. I told you I wanted the iphone.

🔁 Retweeted by Limmy

Expand · ↰ Reply · ⇄ Retweet · ★ Favorite · ••• More

Et Tu, Netflix?

Netflix started as a service that mailed DVDs to subscribers' homes, though most people now associate it with streaming entertainment over the Internet, since "mail" and "DVD" are both things from the ancient past. You'd think that Netflix would be impossible to complain about because it allows subscribers to basically summon anything they want to their screen within seconds, but no. Netflix has a problem: It goes down every now and then.

For most websites, the occasional outage isn't a big deal. People can wait a few minutes to get their banking done on BankOfAmerica.com or order their groceries on FreshDirect.com or solicit an elderly transgendered person to spit on them via Craigslist.org. But Netflix going down is unacceptable. Why is that? Because Netflix delivers higher quality bullshit than even Craigslist—name another place where you can watch 300 *SpongeBob SquarePants* episodes in a row—and First-Worlders love their bullshit. Step between Netflix users and their old episodes of *Veronica Mars* and you're likely to provoke a swarm of extremely irritated tweets. Just like these.

19 hours ago via mobile

Way to go Netflix. Your stupid iphone mobile ads for new series takes you to a trailer stream that is not compatible with iPhones (silverlight).

Like · Comment

👍 2 people like this.

Curse you SILVERLIGHT!!!!
11 hours ago via mobile · Like

Write a comment...

ds
@

Why is my Netflix down I'm on my last season of how I met your mother ☐

↩ Reply ⟲ Retweet ★ Favorite ••• More

The Pains of *Pandora*

In Greek mythology, Pandora opened a box and unleashed into the world all manner of misery and awfulness. And like its namesake, the predictive music service Pandora has opened a box, unleashing an untold number of White Whines into the world. Pandora users complain about anything having to do with the service—not least of which is when the service is unavailable. But nothing seems to rile them up quite like when Pandora's music selection isn't spot-on 100 percent perfect at reading their minds.

First, it's important to know how Pandora works. A Pandora user first picks a song and then, using computer magic created by wealthy nerds, the service selects similar songs to play for the listener. The listener can agree or disagree with the selection, and in this way the Pandora service becomes more and more tailored to the tastes of each individual listener. It seems that this method would make for extremely happy users, but the engineers at Pandora forgot one crucial thing while creating this revolutionary service: People love to complain, especially about things that are (A) new, (B) revolutionary, and (C) free.

"Why is Justin Bieber coming up on my station? I hate his music, and you should have known that about me by now, computer!"

"Hey! How come you're not playing that one song I like by that band I can't remember?! You're stupid, computer!"

"Ugh, hello? This song is clearly acid fusion jazz, so why is it showing up on a playlist that started off with an acid fusion funk song?! Kill yourself, computer!"

Most Pandora White Whiners sadly don't actually call out the computer, as I've done here, but that is basically their intent. They want to shame the computer for its foolish song selection. This makes them White Whiners. Why? Because Pandora is basically a digital DJ whose sole directive is to entertain you with pleasing music tailored to your personal taste, and that sounds pretty First-World to me.

Dylan
20 minutes ago near ▯▯▯▯▯▯▯ via mobile

For the last time pandora, I don't and never will like Coldplay, so stop making me waste my skips!

Like · Comment · Share

Adair ▯▯▯▯
Dear Pandora: When I make a Fleetwood Mac station, I want Fleetwood Mac. Not Tiny FREAKING Dancer. I'm going back to my MGMT station until you get your crap together.
7 minutes ago · Like · Comment

Patrina ▯▯
Thanks a whole lot Pandora for playing Halo even though I told you to never ever play that song again. ughhhhh
6 hours ago · Like · Comment

TUMBLR RANT: so I understand Pandora doesn't work the way you WANT it to but I find it highly annoying that I have the Rihanna station on, and Beyonce plays right after her every time, regardless of whether I thumbs down on the music. You can't tell me that the station hasn't gotten the hint yet. I did the thumbs down button 5, yes, 1, 2, 3, 4.....5 times already and its doing the same thing! UGH. I love Beyonce's music but that's not what I want to hear right now. I wanna hear Rihanna and Rihanna like music.

#done

67890-3452

Too Much *Technology*

I once read about some of our earliest ancestors, called Homo Ergaster, and their favorite tool. Homo Ergaster lived in a valley in Africa, and they made hand axes out of chipped rock. They really loved these hand axes and made them by the thousand. They carried them around, used them to cut meat and skins, and probably ended up smashing each other in the face with them a few times. What's amazing about these hand axes, and a little embarrassing about our ancestors, is that they were happy with the hand ax for a long, long time. Like, hundreds of thousands of years. That was proto-humanity's only technology, and it wasn't changed or improved upon for an unimaginable amount of time. But then someone was like, "Hey, what if we put one of these on a stick, right?" And thus was born the technological society in which we live today.

Technology solves so many problems for us. Before the technological explosion of the last five thousand years, we weren't much better than the apes that climbed down from the trees and gave birth to our species. But now we have harnessed the power of nature to create a stunning array of extremely small, powerful, affordable devices with which to consume an endless variety of pornography. Having multiple devices around at all times leads to its own kind of First-World Problem: Too much technology is kind of annoying.

Dylan
20 minutes ago near [redacted] via mobile

For the last time pandora, I don't and never will like Coldplay, so stop making me waste my skips!

Like · Comment · Share

WhiteWhine

Adair
Dear Pandora: When I make a Fleetwood Mac station, I want Fleetwood Mac. Not Tiny FREAKING Dancer. I'm going back to my MGMT station until you get your crap together.
7 minutes ago · Like · Comment

WhiteWhine

Patrina
Thanks a whole lot Pandora for playing Halo even though I told you to never ever play that song again. ughhhhh
6 hours ago · Like · Comment

WhiteWhine

TUMBLR RANT: so I understand Pandora doesn't work the way you WANT it to but I find it highly annoying that I have the Rihanna station on, and Beyonce plays right after her every time, regardless of whether I thumbs down on the music. You can't tell me that the station hasn't gotten the hint yet. I did the thumbs down button 5, yes, 1, 2, 3, 4.....5 times already and its doing the same thing! UGH. I love Beyonce's music but that's not what I want to hear right now. I wanna hear Rihanna and Rihanna like music.

#done

WhiteWhine

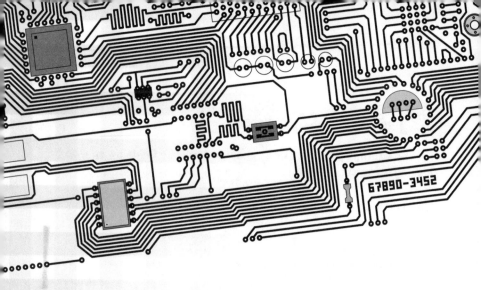

67890-3452

Too Much *Technology*

I once read about some of our earliest ancestors, called Homo Ergaster, and their favorite tool. Homo Ergaster lived in a valley in Africa, and they made hand axes out of chipped rock. They really loved these hand axes and made them by the thousand. They carried them around, used them to cut meat and skins, and probably ended up smashing each other in the face with them a few times. What's amazing about these hand axes, and a little embarrassing about our ancestors, is that they were happy with the hand ax for a long, long time. Like, hundreds of thousands of years. That was proto-humanity's only technology, and it wasn't changed or improved upon for an unimaginable amount of time. But then someone was like, "Hey, what if we put one of these on a stick, right?" And thus was born the technological society in which we live today.

Technology solves so many problems for us. Before the technological explosion of the last five thousand years, we weren't much better than the apes that climbed down from the trees and gave birth to our species. But now we have harnessed the power of nature to create a stunning array of extremely small, powerful, affordable devices with which to consume an endless variety of pornography. Having multiple devices around at all times leads to its own kind of First-World Problem: Too much technology is kind of annoying.

People with abundant amounts of technology are often alerted not once, not twice, but three or four times about the same meeting due to synced devices all doing their job. Plus, the owners of all this technology, our White Whiners, have to find time to use it all. And then of course they have to keep all of those devices charged and updated, which is a job in and of itself. These White Whiners complain that they would be better off if only someone would invent a technology that's entire purpose is to charge and sync all the other technologies! Of course, it goes without saying that these complaints are usually posted to the Internet via the very device(s) the Whiner is complaining about. That's kind of like using a fleet of airplanes to skywrite, "Ugh, maintaining all of these airplanes is so annoying."

You know, sometimes I think our ancestors had it figured out. And then I remember that they all died at 23, probably from a hand axe-related injury.

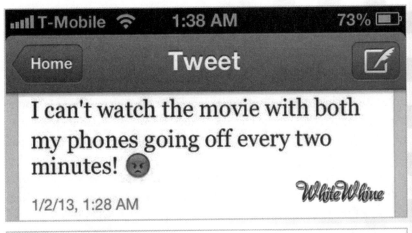

Retail Reactions

Stores, especially national chains, put a great deal of time and money into making customers feel as if the store is their friend. The stores are often personified through professional spokespeople. Or the stores invite you, the consumer, to "come on down" for a visit. It's as if you're being asked to attend a friendly backyard picnic, not aimlessly wander through the Home Depot by the highway looking for whatever a 3" torx screw is. A good number of us fall for the ruse and end up thinking of Home Depot as being our trusted pal. By the highway.

But retailers aren't our pals, are they? They're profit-seeking corporate entities hell-bent on getting as much of your money as they can while spending as little of their own as possible. And in that quest, they will inevitably make changes—they'll redesign the logo, they'll change prices, they'll discontinue certain products, etc. To most people, a new Arby's logo isn't going to evoke any kind of reaction. But to some White Whiners out there, even the smallest change to their favorite store is a personal insult that is aimed squarely at them.

Was it something I did, Bed Bath & Beyond? Because I know you wouldn't discontinue my favorite off-white hand towels for no reason. Does this have anything to do with me and Crate & Barrel? Well, you better get over it, because this new you? Not liking it so much.

To all my fashionistas: why did YSL feel the need to change their name to Saint Laurent Paris all of the sudden??? I mean the Y was on everything. Now all my stuff looks old. LV better not get any ideas!!!!! :/

Like · Comment · 2 minutes ago via mobile ·

I www.whitewhine.com

White Whine – A Collection of First-World Problems
whitewhine.com

A Collection of First-World Problems, Updated Daily

a few seconds ago · Like · Remove Preview

Write a comment...

Really bad news, ladies. Lululemon changed the design of their groove pants. They are now ugly. I'm sooooo disappointed because I have to replace my black pair. Customer service told me that they have no plans to bring the originals back. Time to boycott the brand!

Like · Comment · 16 minutes ago ·

I also resent having to pay more per ounce for a quart sized carton that I didn't want to buy in the first place. It's not like this is a new problem, so why don't the people who order the milk order more of the skim milk, so that when people go to buy the milk it's there! Think of all of the lost revenue on skim milk sales.

9 hours ago · Like · Comment

They usually have the quarts of skim milk, but the quart doesn't have the easy pour spout. So you have to tear open the corner of the carton, which always ends up ripping and then when you're trying to pour milk for your 1am cereal fix, you end up with milk all over your foot.

9 hours ago · Like · Comment

Why is my grocery store always out of the half gallon of skim milk? The shelf is always overflowing with whole milk, chocolate, 1%, 2%... but the skim milk, the milk that most people actually buy, is always out. There's always just an empty space where the half gallons of skim milk should be.

9 hours ago · Like · Comment

My Name Is
Vicki, not *Vicky!*

"My name is my name!" So spake fictional drug kingpin Marlo Stanfield in *The Wire*, a show that I'm confident everyone reading this book has seen. Marlo is stressing the importance of his name regarding the Baltimore heroin trade. But because I've never dealt heroin (in Baltimore), instead I want to talk about the importance of a name regarding something that costs about as much as heroin: Starbucks coffee.

Starbucks has developed an assembly line system for delivering sugary, caffeinated drinks to its loyal customers—that is, every living human being on Earth. Order from the cashier, say your name, pay too much, wait, pick up the world music CD by the register and pretend to consider buying it, hear your name called, and collect your drink. Most people will simply take their drink, glance one more time at the world music CD so everyone knows they're cultured, and then leave. But some people are a little more observant and inspect the cup not only for its contents—with which they'll inevitably find a problem—but for their name. Because most Starbucks cashiers only know one language, plus how to say "small," "medium," and "large" in Italian, they occasionally misspell a customer's name. No big deal, right?

Wrong.

Poor Starbucks customers who are faced with horrible misspellings like "Jenifer" or "Johnathan" or "Mathew," react with a mix of sarcasm and disgust. But really, the sarcasm is only there to mask the disgust they feel that someone who hears and writes down 500 names an hour while making change, pouring coffee, and making sure the register count is accurate could be so stupid as to spell a normal name wrong. A picture of the offending cup will quickly show up on Facebook or Instagram, accompanied by an indignant mini-rant along the lines of "Um, my name is actually spelled "Elissa," not 'Alyssa,' idiot." Charming.

And while you can begin to attempt to start to almost understand why someone would get upset about their name being off by a letter, nothing can prepare your brain for the next level of Starbucks White Whiners: the people who get equally upset because the cashier scribbled the wrong version of their name. On what planet is a person supposed to be able to discern an audible difference between "Sara" and "Sarah," "Steven" and "Stephen," or "Clair" and "Clare"? And don't even get me started on people with names spelled in an "independent" way: the Myke's, Venesza's, Rhobyn's, Jayke's, and Crystofur's of the world. They have no right to chastise anyone besides their parents for misspelling their name, and yet, somehow, they summon the courage to do it anyway.

What's so White Whiney about these people is that they already have their expensive coffee, but they still want you to empathize with their plight. But don't get me wrong; I do feel a great deal of sympathy when I see White Whines like this. Not for the Whiner—who is more upset at a misspelled name on a coffee cup than an Ellis Island immigrant whose legal name has been changed forever—but for the poor Starbucks cashiers who have to deal with these people.

That said, if you spell my name as anything other than "Streeter," you're an idiot. "Street" "er." How hard is that? Seriously . . .

47

Consumer *Retorts*

When you have a lot of money, shopping can be an extremely enjoyable experience (or so I'm told). Apparently, there are people who don't need to shop at outlets, hunt for bargains, or spend their money in a sensible way. We should all be so lucky. Sadly, though, it's apparently not as pleasant as it seems. Even though these White Whiners are rich, they can tap into a well of retail rage as quickly as any redneck accusing a Walmart cashier of "cheatin' 'em outta change." It appears that no matter how high end the store might be, the same complaints apply. And that's what makes these such great White Whines. For example, if I were to say, "This shirt from T. J. Maxx doesn't fit right," it wouldn't really be a White Whine because T. J. Maxx is an affordable store that sells affordable, misstitched, stained clothing in unmarked piles under dead mosquito-filled fluorescent lights (can you tell my mom made me shop at T. J. Maxx a lot as a kid?). However, if I were to say, "I can't find a good tailor who makes bespoke suits that fit my frame," that is a certified White Whine.

And that's what a lot of our sophisticated shoppers are whining about. The whine is not really about the goods they're buying; it's the secondary services that are required to make those goods useable. Shirts have to be tailored, shoes have to be cobbled, and hats have to be haberdashed (that last one may not be accurate). Perhaps that's why they're so angry? They had to spend a ton of money on fashionable clothing and then have to go right back out and spend more money to make that clothing wearable. It's kind of like how you have to spend money on an Xbox and then have to pay to buy all the games. It makes gamers angry, and that's why they all call each other unspeakable names on XBox Live.

But have no fear, there are plenty of White Whines about the clothing itself. Nobody makes anything that fits. Nobody makes anything fashionable. Nobody even carries that one bow tie that I wanted so dearly. If you're complaining about anything having to do with bow ties, Prada, Barneys, or Brooks Brothers, then there's a good chance that you're White Whining.

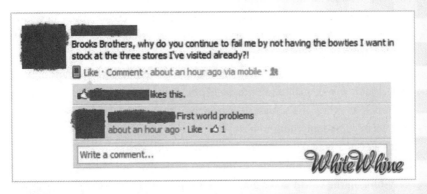

Brooks Brothers, why do you continue to fail me by not having the bowties I want in stock at the three stores I've visited already?!

Like · Comment · about an hour ago via mobile

likes this.

First world problems
about an hour ago · Like · 👍 1

Write a comment...

Ugh, tailoring is expensive. All those J. Crew shirts I got on sale don't seem such a good deal, anymore.

Like · Comment · 14 minutes ago near Clearwater

likes this.

Fancy people problems.
2 seconds ago · Like

Write a comment...

Products, Products Everywhere—And Not a Thing to Buy

This is a wonderful time in history to be a consumer. In times past the only things you could buy were Bibles, livestock, and enslaved human beings. Not our finest hour. But these days the world is positively bursting with things to buy. According to a recent study I just made up, every day China manufactures roughly twenty trillion things that are eagerly bought around the world. And being that there is such a wealth of goods and services available for every consumer, at every price point, it's strange to find people out there who just can't seem to find anything to buy.

It's sad in a way. Their pockets are stuffed with money or credit that they desperately want to pump back into the economy, but they already have everything in the world and cannot find a single thing that they already don't possess. So they travel from store to store, mall to mall, searching, in vain, for something, anything, that they can buy, only to be disappointed by their good fortune over and over again. Even stranger, they believe this is a problem that the world should hear about, and so they complain on Facebook and Twitter. "I already have everything I want," is surely among the great First-World Problems.

I hate it when I have money to spend and can't find anything I want. (@ Target w/ 2 others) 4sq.com/
📄 📍 View summary

Jade
Been shopping for 8 hours spent loads of money & hate every single thing i got!!!
🖥 Like · Comment · about an hour ago near West Parley,

Eileen
I have a slight problem of spending my money on things I know I don't need or will ever use. ugh my life.
Me Gusta · Comment · 56 minutes ago · 👥

👍 2 people gusta this.

Money *for* Nothing

There is almost nothing in this world quite as wonderful as getting free money. You put on your winter jacket, left hanging in the closet since last year, and find $20 crumbled up in the pocket. You go to the ATM to take out $20 and find $40 sitting in the tray, forgotten by some drunken fool who is probably wondering where he lost that $40 he just took out. You might even find a dirty, soggy dollar on a bathroom floor and pocket it without thinking twice. Yes, free money is wonderful, but some White Whiners aren't so easy to please.

The main First-World Problem these White Whiners have with their free payday is that it's just not enough free money, which is insane. That'd be like a woman giving birth to a child only to have her husband complain that he really wanted triplets. Other White Whiners consider the dollar amount of their free money to be "random." Perhaps they suffer from a form of obsessive-compulsive disorder where any monetary gift must be a number that "makes sense." Of course, what makes the most sense when it comes to giving away money is not to give it to White Whiners who will complain about it. But nobody ever said the world was a logical place.

What am I supposed to do with a $50 gift card to Coach? Wipe my ass?

Like · Comment · November 6 at 12:51am near Chicago, IL · 👥

9 people like this.

Luggage tag?
November 6 at 9:12am · Like

Write a comment...

White Whine

Kay
April 5 near Rochester 👥

What am i gonna do with 100 dollars ' my mom make meeh sick -___- GN

Like · Comment

2 people like this.

Write a comment...

White Whine

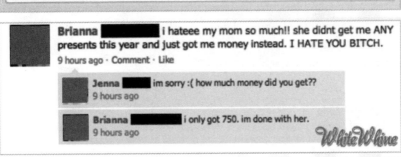

Brianna i hateee my mom so much!! she didnt get me ANY presents this year and just got me money instead. I HATE YOU BITCH.

9 hours ago · Comment · Like

Jenna im sorry :(how much money did you get??
9 hours ago

Brianna i only got 750. im done with her.
9 hours ago

White Whine

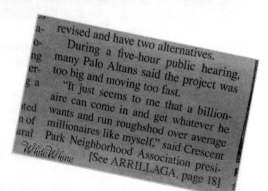

Too Rich

Accumulating wealth is one of the strongest desires we have. It's right up there with sex and not being picked last in gym. Wealth buys security, luxury, peace of mind, and, most importantly, stuff. Most of us will die without ever coming close to achieving the kind of wealth we truly crave. But for a few lucky souls, wealth will be abundant. And they'll kind of hate it.

It seems strange to you and me (unless you're having this book read to you by your butler), but there is a level of wealth where it is a problem. But what kind of problems come with extreme wealth? Well, one of these White Whiners might find that their wallet just isn't big enough to hold all of their money. Or that they're exhausted from going to all of these goddamn formal dinners. There are even hazards to one's safety, such as living in a house with a ton of chandeliers in an earthquake-prone area or getting stuck inside their own personal elevator.

As you can see, these are problems that the regular well-off aspire to have. Perhaps no amount of writing I could do could capture these White Whines as poetically and succinctly as the late Notorious B.I.G. when he truthfully declared, "Mo' money, mo' problems."

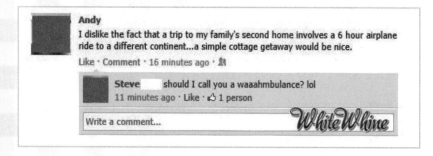

Andy
I dislike the fact that a trip to my family's second home involves a 6 hour airplane ride to a different continent...a simple cottage getaway would be nice.
Like · Comment · 16 minutes ago ·

> **Steve** ___ should I call you a waaahmbulance? lol
> 11 minutes ago · Like · 👍 1 person

Write a comment...

WhiteWhine

Something wrong with this country when in the space of 4 months we pay $60,000 in freaking TAXES. FOUR MONTHS, not a year or more. Rather than support lazy freeloaders, we could really use the money to pay student loans or put in college savings or life savings or or or.. You get the point.

Like · Comment · 6 hours ago near Salmon Creek, WA

Dennis

Been a customer of starbucks for years probably spent thousands of dollars on there coffee over the course of that time and have always been a happy customer.... Until today when I was sent away because I only had a 100.00 bill waited in line to be told we can't take your cash... They didn't even try to break it what a joke I'm about to boycott .... Great customer service !!!!

Like · Comment · February 26 at 6:32pm via mobile

👍 2 people like this.

midnight full-moonlight salt-bath left water in my ear =(

Like · Comment · 6 minutes ago · ✖

    Rachel   are you vying for a spot on whitewhine.com?
    about a minute ago · Like

Toby

Is stuck in his own elevator...how embarassing...

    22 June at 14:42 via Friendly for iPad · Like · Comment · Get Friendly

👍   and 18 others like this.

    Sasha   LOL
    22 June at 14:43 · Like · 👍1 person

gone from pasta and pesto and tennents for three weeks at uni, to caviar on toast, smoked salmon sandwiches, and red wine at home. don't think my body can handle such rich food.

Like · Comment · 32 minutes ago · ✳

👍 2 people like this.

    Write a comment...

Checks and Imbalances

Once, long ago, people paid for things with checks. Checks were little pieces of paper on which you would be forced to write the name of the payee, the dollar amount in longhand, the date, and, finally, your scribble on the bottom to prove that it was really your check (since every scribble is unique to the scribbler). Checks have fallen out of favor in recent years because we've found faster, easier, less-stupid ways to spend money. But there are still people out there using them. And every place you find someone writing a check, you'll find an annoyed White Whiner waiting behind them.

What's so frustrating to these White Whiners is the eons it takes for someone to write out a check. Unlike a tap or a swipe or even a cash transaction, a check can take up to forty seconds to write. Forty seconds?! Who has that kind of time these days? Why, if that jerk at the front of the line had just put it on a card like a normal human, we could already be on our way to the ski house in Vermont by now!

But what makes these annoyed shoppers such great White Whiners is what lies at the core of their complaint. Underneath the moaning about waiting in line and how they picked the wrong lane is a person who is basically asking, "How come it's taking so long for me to spend my money?!"

Is there a more pure First-World Problem than that?

White Whine

Spotting lane stoppers is key. I try avoid standing behind old people (they love writing checks), poor people (foodstamps), and coupon clippers.

Stewart ▮▮▮▮▮▮ ✕
Checkbook at the supermarket? In the express lane?!?

FML!

📱 5 hours ago via iPhone · Like · Comment

> **Njer**▮▮▮▮ do you do your grocery shopping in 1987?? good luck with that! :)
> 5 hours ago · Like

> **Stewart** ▮▮▮▮▮ He was a Member's Only jacket away from being an extra in Magnum PI.
> 4 hours ago · Like

> **Andrew**▮▮▮▮ My favorite is when someone is in the 15 items or less line with 30+ items, then throws huge fit until they check him out anyways. Because after all, he couldn't read the sign. Happened other day at stop and shop. Thank god for personal checkout lanes.
> 4 hours ago · Like

> **Jeff** ▮▮▮▮ http://whitewhine.com/
> 17 seconds ago · Like

Write a comment...

WhiteWhine

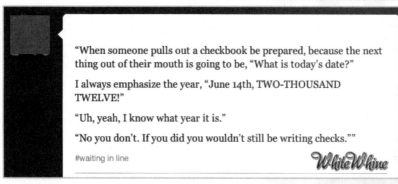

"When someone pulls out a checkbook be prepared, because the next thing out of their mouth is going to be, "What is today's date?"

I always emphasize the year, "June 14th, TWO-THOUSAND TWELVE!"

"Uh, yeah, I know what year it is."

"No you don't. If you did you wouldn't still be writing checks.""

#waiting in line

WhiteWhine

E ▮▮▮▮ ▮ 👤▾ 🐦 Follow
@ ▮▮▮▮ ▮

If you spend $127 on 12 items in the express lane and then write a check, i hope you get acidic diarrhea.

↩ Reply 🔁 Retweet ★ Favorite ••• More

WhiteWhine

An *Embarrassment* by Riches

I'm embarrassed by a lot of things. I don't like dancing, especially when other people are in the room or watching me in any way. I don't particularly enjoy the thirty extra pounds of chub my body is wearing. And I failed the presidential fitness test every year because I couldn't sit-and-reach to the President's exacting standard (which, for the record, is total bullshit. The sit-and-reach being on a fitness test is like having a hot dog eating contest on the SATs). One thing I have sadly never been embarrassed by is the amount of money I have. There are two reasons for this: One, I don't have that much money and two, I can't imagine ever being embarrassed by having money since, ya know, other than love and children, it's kind of the one nonessential thing we're all after.

But there are those in the world for whom money, or any outward display of money, is a great source of shame. Like the Yankee blue bloods of yesteryear, the insecure rich today shy away from their wealth while simultaneously letting everyone know that they're definitely super rich. But instead of donating hospital wings or funding libraries like in olden times, now they just post online about how nobody understands how mortifying it is to be a .00001-percenter. They don't like to drive expensive cars because people gawk. They don't want to bring their pricey handbags to school because nobody else can afford them. Some, God help them, don't even like riding in limos. In limos! The most fun kind of car to ride in!

Like any White Whine, there's a degree of "Are you kidding me?" when you come across someone who is complaining about their vast wealth. But it's worth keeping in mind that many of these Whiners here didn't even make this money themselves. It was cruelly and carelessly forced upon them by family members or trust fund managers, all without their consent and sometimes even their knowledge. It's a shameful world where people can be forced to be rich against their will—or by benefit of a dead grandfather's will, I suppose—and I, for one, won't stand for it. That's why I am offering here, in these pages, my services. Anyone embarrassed by their fortune may give it to me and relieve themselves of the awful burden of having more than everyone else.

How the Other "Half" "Lives"

One of the many benefits of being incredibly wealthy is that you can live out your entire life without having to really deal with people who aren't disgustingly rich. You can fly private to avoid normals on commercial flights. You can live in gated communities to avoid less affluent neighbors. You can send your children to expensive private schools to dodge the painful reality that not everyone's family owns enough Coca-Cola stock to be permitted to know the secret formula. I once heard about a billionaire who had never been to a grocery store. And why should he? Food—like clothing, Christmas gifts, and sex—just appeared when he wanted it, so why bother learning where it came from? There are more important things to do, like go swimming in a pool of gold coins. But every now and then even the most wealthy and cultured among us must mix with the hoi polloi, and this confluence of the River Rich and the Poor Puddle creates some wonderfully classicist White Whines.

Rich First-Worlders find themselves shocked, appalled, and, mostly, frustrated that not only people could live in such a manner but that they themselves are being forced to experience it, too. A trip to Walmart is met with disdain and fear. The ragged rabble at Dunkin' Donuts is shunned and impolitely asked to vacate the premises. Car mechanics are barely tolerated, not for their shoddy workmanship but for their horrid appearance. The vibe I pick up from all of these White Whines is that a poor rich person has stumbled upon America's dirty secret—that not everyone is a refined, rarified captain of industry—and they're reporting back to the other aristocrats about the shameful sights they've seen.

Like modern day Jacob Riises, these brave First-Worlders have descended into the depths of the middle class and do not like what they see. Perhaps one of these White Whiners will be so moved by the abject normalness so rampant in this country that they will start a reform movement. But more likely they'll just return to their gated mansions as quickly as possible, get on Facebook, and warn the others about the kind of ingrates who frequent our nation's grocery stores.

 Dylan
3 hours ago via mobile

The majority of our lives Martha and I are rarely around 'normal' people since we don't shop at Wal-Mart or eat fast-food. Wow, normal is scary!

Like · Comment

 Martha   I don't want to be snobby or anything, but there is a reason why we need to support education, plant based diets, and progressive legislation. Dylan, there better be clean needles here and I better not get some kind of weird trailer park germ.
3 hours ago via mobile · Like

Getting new tires on the jag. Everyone here has greasy ponytails and lumberjack beards. Kill myself — at Cassidy tire shop.

1 hour ago

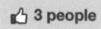 3 people

Whole Foods' *Bold Fools*

Whole Foods is a national chain of "progressive" grocery stores that caters to America's most finicky eaters. They're known for their large selection of organic, fair trade, free range, cruelty free, sustainable, and green products. They're also known for their White Whiney customers.

Level 1 Whole Foods White Whiners take issue with the store's general attributes. For instance, the complicated Whole Foods checkout line process leaves many a customer fuming because it takes them literally minutes longer to haul their artisanal gorp out to their car. Other customers have a problem with the store's high prices, though I'm sure they'd be just as upset if the store was cheap, because shopping there would no longer be a status symbol.

But my favorite Whole Foods White Whiners are at Level 2, which involves taking issue with the actual products available in the store. There's just something hysterical to me about someone who can be worked into a rage because Whole Foods uses canola oil in something instead of olive oil or because they haven't properly sliced the grapefruit in the salad bar into small enough chunks.

Of course at the end of the day any complaint about Whole Foods is a First-World Problem because it takes a First-World income to even afford to complain about Whole Foods.

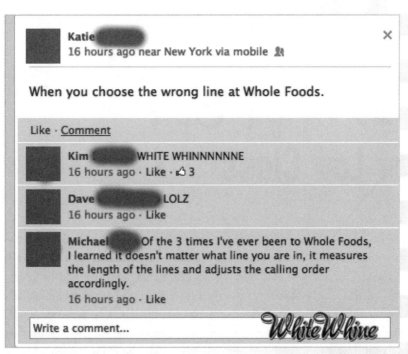

Katie
16 hours ago near New York via mobile

When you choose the wrong line at Whole Foods.

Like · Comment

Kim WHITE WHINNNNNE
16 hours ago · Like · 👍 3

Dave LOLZ
16 hours ago · Like

Michael Of the 3 times I've ever been to Whole Foods,
I learned it doesn't matter what line you are in, it measures
the length of the lines and adjusts the calling order
accordingly.
16 hours ago · Like

Write a comment...

White Whine

Follow

Was about to pay for a ton of groceries at
Whole Foods.. then got evacuated for a fire
$@#! Freshdirect is starting to look
appealing.

Reply   Retweet   Favorite

5:13 PM - 13 Jan 13 · Embed this Tweet

Reply to   *White Whine*

SouthBronxUnite @SouthBronxUnite   9h
please consider impact of using FreshDirect:
1,000 daily truck trips through South Bronx n'hood with asthma
rates 8X nat'l ave
Details

Pity Add—♫♥... @fydzatwit   now
@whitewhines alert!
Details Reply Delete Favorite

© 2013 Twitter About Help

The *High Cost* of Low Class

I believe it was Benjamin Franklin—renowned inventor of the Franklin stove—who once quipped, "In this world nothing can be said to be certain except death and taxes." Franklin should have added, "And also that there will be people who complain about having to pay their taxes." Granted, my amendment isn't as catchy, but it is just as true. For every tax, there will be someone loudly complaining about it. It's pretty much what started America going in the first place, and we haven't changed our tune that much (though it is getting harder to find tea to dump into the ocean). Most people will grumble about their taxes and then pay up because they like having things like working fire departments, highways that aren't crumbling, a strong standing army, social security for when they get old, and public schools to teach their children about the complicated tax system in America (and that they'll grow up to complain about themselves someday). But there is a group of White Whiners who seem to be fine with the concept of taxation, just not where the tax money is going. Specifically, they're not happy that their taxes are going to help the less fortunate.

I think the major problem for these people is a disconnect between how they imagined the tax system working and how it actually works. To them, taxes are money that is set aside for them to spend on federal projects that they agree with. For this specific group of people I imagine those projects would be things like building giant golden statues of themselves or paving the highways with diamonds so that the approach to the giant golden statues is just as impressive as the statues themselves. What they didn't realize is that taxes usually go to programs that help everyone, not just entitled, empathy-less, selfish, garbage people like them. Some will hide behind statements like "I'm fiscally conservative but socially liberal," which translated from bullshit into English reads, "I support poor people's right to exist, but I'm not about to help any of them." They can of course vote for politicians whose tax policies align more closely with their own interests, but pro-diamond road candidates are few and far between.

If you happen to be one of these people, I think it would be a good idea for you to protest these wasteful programs by refusing to pay your taxes this year. And next year, too. And then one day the government will come scoop you up and deposit you in prison for tax evasion. And only then, finally, will you too get to live for free off the taxpayer's dime and experience just how good those less fortunate people have it!

46 minutes ago near Tucson, AZ · 🌐

Today showed me exactly why Obama can go fuck himself and is a worthless piece of shit. You support the homeless and needy who yelled and threatened my life today for getting in a range rover telling me I was worthless and worth nothing in life. Hope you realize people commit suicide off such cruel accusations, judging me off the items my family bought me who work their ass off everyday and donate their money they earn to multiple foundations. My dad came from nothing and became a top doctor on his own earning his own money working 3 jobs graduating top 10% of his class and going to medical school for over fucking 12 years of his life to be where he is today. While, on the other hand, all you do is mooch off people for money and say cruel things to people to give you money to go buy drugs and continue to do nothing with your life. That is your problem not mine and I will have no sympathy for people like you because my dad is a prime example of someone who had nothing and became something prooving anyone can be who they want by something you probably have never heard of that is called "working". You tell me I am nothing when I am attending a university in order to go to law school to make something of myself while your sitting on your ass begging me for money my dad has given me and has well earned and deserved. Makes total sense to support such soulless individuals? So please do not tell me I am worthless you lazy piece of shit. Anyone that supports such a human being can go fuck yourself with him just as well. Please try and refute my statement fucking laze betches because anyone can be anything they aspire. Fuck you Obama! I hope you get what you deserve in this presidential election you fucking terrorist alien devil. You are the most worthless individual I have ever met and are an enemy to America and to people who have well earned the money they deserve. #NOBAMATILLIDIE

Like · Comment · Share

👍 9 people like this.

this is the most ignorant status in the world
37 minutes ago · Like · 👍 48

White Whine

This comment has received too many negative votes
If only these goddamn socialists didnt bother me. My parents can pay for Exeter, Harvard , and a Stanford grad school education. Get govt. off my ass! Fuzz you poor people, learn to work hard! Do you even have any idea how much time I have to spend every morning thinking about stock prices!!!! Yeah now thats work, learn some!
1 week ago

White Whine

Pining for Poverty

You know how recipients of organ transplants often long for the halcyon days when their old heart or kidneys didn't work? Of course not, because that is a stupid desire to have. And yet some White Whiners find themselves strangely pining for simpler times—even if those times never existed—when they didn't have all this stupid money to worry about.

Oh, to be poor again! Life was so much easier (it wasn't)! Experiences were so much richer (they weren't)! Life was one big adventure back then (if by "adventure" you mean "terrifying slog from one paycheck to the next," then yes, it was). Yearning for poorer days is as strange as longing to go back to getting bullied in middle school all over again.

Even stranger are Whiners who think that posting about their desire for a return to poverty will somehow not make poorer people hate them even more. Maybe these White Whiners see themselves as Gandhi-like figures who, by throwing off the trappings of the modern world, would find peace and happiness. And maybe they would if they did actually throw off the trappings of the modern world, but they don't, and so they won't. They just want the nostalgia, not the canned beans from the dollar store for dinner.

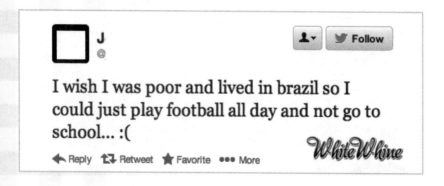

J
@

1▾ 🐦 Follow

I wish I was poor and lived in brazil so I could just play football all day and not go to school... :(

← Reply ⇄ Retweet ★ Favorite ••• More

WhiteWhine

about an hour ago near Charleston, SC

i miss being poor. i miss scrounging up all the change i could find, just so i could get a red bull from wawa and then put two bucks in the gas tank just so i could drive to yorktown beach. i miss virginia beach, and surfing at 1st street and croatan, especially in the winter. i miss virginia.

Me gusta · Comment · Unfollow post · Share

9 people like this.

Girl, I feel you. :(
52 minutes ago · Me gusta

Don't ever miss being poor,be thankful for where you are and what you have,I miss all those things too!
27 minutes ago via Mobile · Me gusta

being poor was nice. more money more problems. when we didnt have anything, we never focused on so much, like we do now. it was much much simpler times.
22 minutes ago · Me gusta

Smart girl.
10 minutes ago · Me gusta

http://whitewhine.com/

White Whine - A Collection of First-World Problems
whitewhine.com
A Collection of First-World Problems, Updated Daily

A few seconds ago · Me gusta · Remove preview

Write a comment...

White Whine

Criminal *Negligence*

Robberies happen all the time, everywhere, and there's nothing anyone can do about it. Why? Because people like to take each other's stuff. But robbery has also led to a couple of the oddest White Whines I've seen come into the site. These episodes star robbery victims who are not upset that they've been fleeced, but are upset that the thief didn't have better taste.

Why not take the money and the expensive wallet? Why not use the stolen credit card to dine at a fancy restaurant? Why not live a little bit, Mr. Criminal?

Sabrina *WhiteWhine*

To whoever stole my wallet and charged lunch at Cosi to my visa, why wouldn't you splurge and go to Pod? Your taste is as bad as your karma. Enjoy my beautiful wallet

Mari

Why would someone steal only $15 out of a wallet that has over $80, not take my Starbucks card, credit cards, or the wallet that is worth over $150? This doesn't seem right.

Like · Comment · 2 hours ago · 👥

> **Taylor** They're a nice thief who doesn't like Starbucks?
> 37 minutes ago · Like

> **Waleed** ....Are you really complaining that a thief didn't steal enough from you?
> a few seconds ago · Like

> |Write a comment... *WhiteWhine*

Taylor   ✕
7 hours ago near Portland 👥

WHO are these car thieves stealing designer dog bags out of cars and LEAVING stereos?! Seriously, this is the SECOND TIME someone has taken Wyatt's dog pouch and left my top of the line stereo/iphone cable.

Like · Comment · Share   *WhiteWhine*

Taylor is there a black market somewhere? How can I get in on that because I REALLY don't want to pay to buy a new one (again)
7 hours ago · Like

···

Taylor just thought they had small dogs and really good taste
7 hours ago · Like · 👍5

···

Katherine When my car was stolen a similar thing happened to me!! When it was found the stereo and CD's were left but Lucy's dirty blanket, pillow and collar was missing! I had just gone shopping and they took my new bag of dog food and detergent as well... But left a Mormon ceremonial gown? Weird.
5 hours ago via mobile · Like

Taylor ...why did you have a Mormon ceremonial gown in your car? Hahah ✕ weirdo.
4 hours ago · Like

I Swear, *Some People*

My mother once brought home a VHS tape (so this was a while ago) about manners, and then forced my family to watch it. The video featured a stuffy old British lady who was, I believe, the last living Victorian, and four or five ethnically diverse kids who were to be instructed about how to properly act better than everyone else. The old lady seemed to lean on a little black boy particularly hard, leading my dad to declare the video racist, leading my sister and I to pop it out, throw it in the back yard, and shoot it with a BB gun while my mom yelled about how she didn't want to raise a family of barbarians. It is one of my fondest memories and one that informs our next little batch of White Whiners: people who cannot come to terms with the fact that not everyone went to finishing school.

With seven billion people walking around on this world of ours, everyone is sure to find someone whose rude ways they see as an affront to organized society. Where you and I differ from the White Whiners (hopefully) is that you or I do not feel the need to chastise someone in print or to their face when we detect a breach of what we believe to be a societal code of conduct. White Whiners feel no such urge to hold their tongue (which, if you were to actually do it, is a fairly rude and strange gesture).

A door not being held is enough to provoke a reaction from the etiquette police. Wearing knockoff fashion is an insult to the designers, and they won't stand for it! Even something as arcane as not knowing the proper rules for attending a symphony can make a White Whiner boil over with rage.

It must be hard for these Whiners to live in a world where the slightest breach of etiquette causes them to take out their phone and compose a little rant on the subject. It has to be difficult to maintain that level of annoyance day in and day out. Plus, constantly typing on your phone is a fairly rude thing to do, causing others nearby to whine about how "people need to learn to put their phones away at the theatre," feeding into this absurd notion that there is only one "acceptable" way to behave, eventually leading some wrinkly old British racist to make a video about manners that my mom will force me to watch.

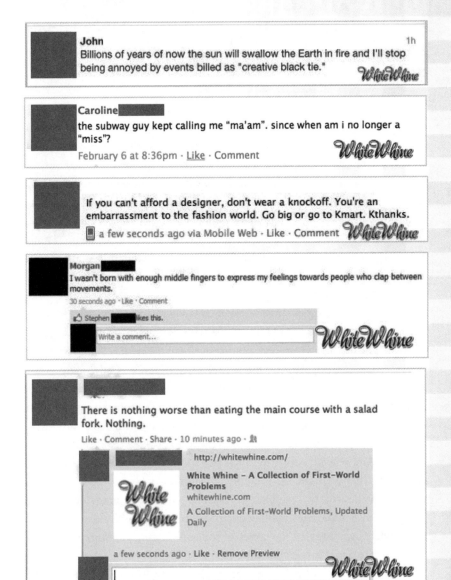

John 1h
Billions of years of now the sun will swallow the Earth in fire and I'll stop being annoyed by events billed as "creative black tie."

Caroline
the subway guy kept calling me "ma'am". since when am i no longer a "miss"?
February 6 at 8:36pm · Like · Comment

If you can't afford a designer, don't wear a knockoff. You're an embarrassment to the fashion world. Go big or go to Kmart. Kthanks.
a few seconds ago via Mobile Web · Like · Comment

Morgan
I wasn't born with enough middle fingers to express my feelings towards people who clap between movements.
30 seconds ago · Like · Comment
Stephen likes this.
Write a comment...

There is nothing worse than eating the main course with a salad fork. Nothing.
Like · Comment · Share · 10 minutes ago ·

http://whitewhine.com/
White Whine – A Collection of First-World Problems
whitewhine.com
A Collection of First-World Problems, Updated Daily
a few seconds ago · Like · Remove Preview

Be Neither
Seen Nor Heard

Since the very beginning of civilization, wealthier people have found that their housework could be greatly reduced, if not eliminated altogether, by investing in cheap labor saving devices: other people. Help—in the noun form of the word, that is—is one of the great aspirations for anyone who hates to live in, and also clean, their home. This is pretty much everyone. And while it's nice to have someone else de-tiger-stripe the toilet (while accusing them of stealing jewelry), having help around the house is often a source of immense trauma for those lucky enough to afford it. Why? Because the hired help are people, too. And people make noises, get up early, and, shockingly, cannot read the minds of their employers.

All kinds of domestics—maids, cleaning ladies, landscapers—play starring roles in White Whines uttered by people who don't seem to realize that (A) we're living in the twenty-first century and (B) *Downton Abbey* is make believe. One of their favorite things to complain about is how early in the morning domestics start their work, which seems like a weird thing for an employer to be annoyed by. In no other business would the boss get mad at the employee for coming to work early. "This goddamn grill cook I just hired. He's here at 7 A.M., getting all the dishes ready and baking the bread! What an asshole!" And when it comes to things like vacuuming, mowing the lawn, or retiling a new bathroom, the ideal time to start work seems to be "when I'm already awake, you fucking ingrate!" What's particularly funny about these White Whines is that they're often composed from bed, where the author has been rudely awakened by the noises of someone else making sure their life is as comfortable and easy as possible.

These Whiners can be somewhat forgiven, however, because no matter who you are, how much money you have, or how kind a person you may be otherwise, if you're awoken by a vacuum on a Saturday morning you're going to act like a complete anus. A second, decidedly more aristocratic set, however, can't seem to grasp the notion that being completely invisible is impossible for hired help. This brand of White Whiner wants to have his cake and eat it too, so long as he doesn't have to see his private chef bake it or his butler bring it to the table. Also, the fact that the help might need to do something like make a phone call or use the bathroom is considered a monstrous breach of protocol, as if the homeowner's toilet will be damaged should it encounter lesser shit.

It's easy to get twisted up in an angry ball when you come across someone complaining about the help. But you really should try to temper your annoyance. If a person feels free to openly complain about and/or insult their domestics in public, imagine how they treat those same domestics in the confines of their own home. But on the plus side, imagine the indescribably disgusting things those domestics do to their employers' toothbrushes. That should make you feel better.

15 hours ago near Dubai 🏠

So, it turns out my maid has never heard of the concept of cereal for when i told her about making cereal, she brings me the bowl, with the cereal without milk, so i tell her to bring it with milk as well which i thought she probably just forgot... she brings the milk in a separate glass...

Like · Comment

6 people like this.

WhiteWhine

First world problems...
14 hours ago via mobile · Like · 👍 1

meh, its not as bad as that one time my old maid brought me cereal, she did it all correct, the bowl, with the cereal inside and the cereal was floating in good old white milk, but why the fuck did she find it necessary to boil the milk first?
14 hours ago · Like · 👍 1

reply   reblog   ♥

The Bosnians are still here and they are still working

it is after 5

dont you have something better to do than work on my kitchen?

Im getting hungry....

WhiteWhine

73

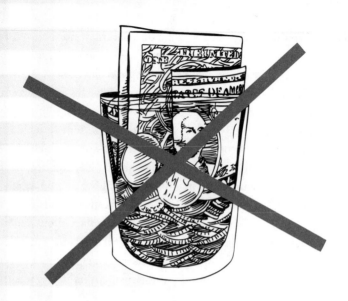

No Tip *for You*

If movies and TV are to be believed, when a medieval king did not feel he was being treated properly by an underling he would bellow, "Off with his head!" and a horde of sycophants would whisk the unlucky fellow away to meet God. The days of lopping off the heads of underperforming servants are long gone, but that doesn't mean the idea of shaming someone lower on the social ladder for poor service has disappeared. These days, the customer is king, and the way he expresses his displeasure is by lopping percentages off a waiter's tip.

Normally, a 20 percent tip is considered fair for good service, but tips get slashed for any number of minor infractions. Sometimes a customer isn't happy with how he or she has been treated and snips a little off. Sometimes a customer isn't pleased with the food—which, obviously, the waiter doesn't have anything to do with—and trims a little bit more. In rare cases, a customer can be against the entire concept of waiters, and so slashes the tip just to let the wait staff know that the whole institution is ridiculous.

Having spent a good amount of my teenage years waiting on people, I know the life of a waiter well. It's a depressing march from one insult to the next—from a customer who wants "colder lettuce" to a line cook who refuses to learn your name and instead only calls you "little homo." The only light at the end of this long, dark tunnel of abuse is a wad of crumpled bills. If those bills are denied, waiters can be among the most spiteful, evil people in the world. Should you ever return to a restaurant where you stiffed a waiter and get that waiter again, you'll find that for every percent you left off of a tip, you'll get an equivalent amount of spit, dishwater, and line-cook sneeze added to your meal. On the house, of course.

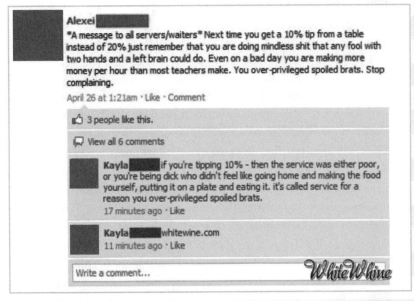

Alexei
A message to all servers/waiters Next time you get a 10% tip from a table instead of 20% just remember that you are doing mindless shit that any fool with two hands and a left brain could do. Even on a bad day you are making more money per hour than most teachers make. You over-privileged spoiled brats. Stop complaining.
April 26 at 1:21am · Like · Comment

👍 3 people like this.

💬 View all 6 comments

> **Kayla** if you're tipping 10% - then the service was either poor, or you're being dick who didn't feel like going home and making the food yourself, putting it on a plate and eating it. it's called service for a reason you over-privileged spoiled brats.
> 17 minutes ago · Like

> **Kayla** whitewine.com
> 11 minutes ago · Like

Write a comment...

White Whine

Amanda
My pedicurist just got up and walked away.... No tip fo you
Like · Comment · Share · about an hour ago near Cape Coral ·

👍 and 3 others like this.

White Whine

Don't You Be My Neighbor

Neighbors are what results from not having enough money to buy a private island. Almost everyone has neighbors, and normally they're great to have around. They'll lend you a cup of sugar if you're in need. They'll sign for a UPS package that only seems to show up when you're out. And if you're bored, they might entertain you with loud sex noises. We all strive to be courteous to those living nearby, but sometimes there's a White Whiner in the neighborhood. And nothing you do will ever convince that White Whiner that you should be allowed to share a square mile of land with them.

White Whiners can find fault in almost anything their neighbors do. Outdoor decorations are a blight on the neighborhood. The noise coming from the neighbor's house is inexcusable. Even the neighborhood kids being too fat is a cause for complaint. There's no pleasing the White Whine family down the street, no matter how much weight little Tyler loses.

Now let me tell you a quick story about why I love White Whiney neighbors. There was a couple who bought a huge old colonial house near my hometown in Connecticut. Their new neighbors threw the young couple a housewarming party when they moved in. The old house needed a new paint job, and the topic of color came up. The snooty residents scoffed when the new homeowners said they were thinking about painting the house blue. "Blue," the snoots said, "is not a proper color for a colonial house." Instead of bowing to the demands of their new neighbors, the young couple painted their new house a different primary color on each side, much to the chagrin of the snoots next door.

And this is why I love White Whiney neighbors: because they always get what's coming to them, be it a multicolored house, even more outdoor decorations, even later-night parties, or even fatter neighborhood kids. It's fun to keep up with the Joneses, but it's even more fun to piss them off, I guess.

76

GOD. i wish my neighbor didnt have fat kids... cause every damn afternoon the Ice Cream truck comes through the neighborhood with that annoying music. The ice cream truck driver -being the business man that he is- knows where allllll dem fat kids at, parks, and waits. $#@&!

Like · Comment · Share

👍 2 people like this.

WhiteWhine

Will

To whoever is staying in the chalet next to mine at Center Parcs Eifel... if you spend all night tonight shouting like you did last night, until 5am when some of us have to work the next day, I am going to fill your car's grill with camembert so that when you turn the ignition on your fucking shitty mercedes will smell like arse. Got it?

July 23 at 2:18am · Like · Comment

WhiteWhine

So, I guess when the infiltration of Indians in my apartment complex draw creepy symbols outside their front door and leave unattended candles burning in the breezeways all night it's considered freedom of religion. But aside from the fact that my son has been waking up hysterical in the middle of the night during this event that invites some goddess into their homes during the new moon, I am sure someone would find a reason to be "offended" if I put my Christmas tree in the breezeway with crosses and Scripture posted. It's different for us, right? Oh yeah.

Like · Comment · 21 hours ago near Richmond ·

👍 4 people like this.

> Tell it like it is, and don't let anything move u!
> 20 hours ago · Like

> Yeah u should do that cuz ur breezeway would look way cooler than theirs too
> 19 hours ago · Like

> Go Amber!! I'll come help you decorate it if you do it. Haha
> 18 hours ago · Like

Write a comment...

WhiteWhine

Customer *Disservice*

Sometimes I walk around and marvel at how many people in this world exist to serve us. Almost anything I need can be brought, performed, cooked, or created for me for a small fee. And for things that I don't need, but oh so badly want, there is someone on Craigslist who will get it (or do it) for $35 and not ask any questions. We're all basically living like Roman emperors in this modern world. That being the case, it's no surprise that a few people out there are none too pleased with the service that their eminence has received. Only instead of throwing people to the lions, these days an offended royal only needs to head to the Internet to make their displeasure known.

Sometimes the complaints are legitimate, if still White Whiney. The barista made the wrong drink. The bagel isn't properly cream cheesed. The person on the customer service line has a southern accent. These are all reasonable things to get upset and complain about. But then some White Whiners take a step off the reasonable trail most of us walk and run headlong down insane lane.

The more "colorful" customer service White Whines involve finding fault with everything from a mentally challenged person bagging groceries incorrectly to a waiter seating them at anything but the best table to my personal favorite, the BMW dealership not having free cookies and a golf simulator like the Lexus dealership does. The "am I being reasonable" filter has been completely removed from their personas, leaving them only with unrealistic demands, unrelenting criticism, and un-fucking-believably funny rants about how much they hate olive cream cheese.

Liz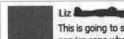
This is going to sound incredibly ... classist ... but I don't like talking to customer service reps who have southern accents. There. I said it.

Me Gusta · Comment · 8 hours ago ·

👍 3 people gusta this.

> **Morgan**  Really? Those ones are my favorite! They always sound so cheerful, and like they honestly want to help.
> 7 hours ago · Me Gusta · 👍 1
>
> **Liz** They sound to me very ingenuine. And dumb and I don't feel helped so much as annoyed bc I think they won't do anything.
> 7 hours ago via mobile · Me Gusta

Write a comment...

White Whine

Christopher
The retarded girl who bagged my groceries did a really terrible job.

📱 3 hours ago via Android · 🔒 · Like · Comment

👍 Huger likes this.

Write a comment...

White Whine

---

facebook   Search for people, places and

@ BMW dealership for oil change. Turned off the tv b/c watching food network w/ commercials is sorta like hell. 3 employees have asked me if I want it turned on! The answer---NO! What I want is for you to make chocolate chip cookies for me and let me play with the golf simulator like I used to at Lexus. They are lucky their car is faster!

Like · Comment · about an hour ago via mobile ·

👍 2 people like this.

White Whine

Waiter *Haters*

I remember learning about the Indian caste system in school. Up top were the priests (obviously), followed by the warriors (who probably could have taken that top spot if they really wanted), then the traders (who were too busy counting rupees to care about this whole thing), and finally, down at the bottom of the barrel, were the workmen (just like today!). Then there were people who were not included in the caste system. These people were the untouchables and, as their name implies, they weren't fit for touching (or talking to or helping or seeing or anything else, really). Our modern world has done away with institutionalized castes in favor of informal ones, but we haven't gotten rid of the untouchables. They're still there, only these days we call them waiters.

That's not entirely true for everyone, of course. Some people treat waiters with the dignity and respect that every human life deserves. But then there are people who look at waiters like steaming piles of trash who saunter over to the table and start screaming something about the specials. Some people just can't seem to bring themselves to treat waiters like anything resembling a human being, it seems; and since a waiter is basically a servant slave that you share with everyone else at Denny's, complaining about one is a certified White Whine.

How do you feel when waiters/waitresses/bartenders/baristas automatically start your "usual" without asking you first? What if you want to try something new, and they get irritated when you tell them? ("but you always get the grande skinny vanilla latte!")

Like · Comment · Friday at 1:02pm ·

 I so rarely order the same thing, they always wait to hear what it is I want today. :)
Friday at 1:03pm · Like

 They should never be snippy about anything to your face, ever. That's bad customer service. It's sweet that they want to make your life easier by getting things started, but they can't be rude about it when that backfires.
Friday at 1:17pm · Like

 Yeah, they think that remembering your "usual" is good customer service, but when they get snippy about it, then it turns into bad customer service. My theory is that they like to keep things as simple as possible, and they're thrown for a loop when you "complicate" things (i.e., order a holiday drink instead of your usual skinny vanilla, or a Chardonnay instead of an appletini).
Friday at 1:32pm · Like

 HUGE HUGE pet peeve of mine
Friday at 2:58pm · Like

Write a comment...

Sean

It's as if "medium rare" doesn't mean anything anymore

about an hour ago via iPhone · Unlike · Comment

@

I've never met a waiter happy to redeem a foursquare special. Utter disdane everytime.

2 minutes ago via Mobile Web ☆ Favorite ♺ Retweet ↻ Reply

Yelp, That Was Terrible

Yelp is a popular social review site used by millions of amateur critics every day to White Whine about local businesses. Users can rate a business and then offer lengthy essays about why they're "never fuking going bak here ever!" or how "the employies here r rude an fat." Not surprisingly, restaurants are often subject to the most scathing Yelp reviewers. More often than not, the complaint has nothing to do with the "desent food" and instead has everything to do with the "experience."

I can't tell you how many Yelp reviews rant and rage about a restaurant's lack of service, ugly decor, room temperature, long wait, ugly coat check girl, complicated menu, small bathroom, high prices, poor music, loud music, lack of music, overcrowding, dim lights, bright lights . . . you get the idea . . . while concluding with a short nod to the delicious food. This is like visiting a prostitute and complaining about the ugly motel room, the lack of HBO on the motel TV, the rude motel clerk, and the blood stains all over the carpet. "But how was the sex?" the policeman would ask as he helps you into the back of the cruiser.

"The sex?" you ask.

"Yeah. I mean, you talked a lot about the place where the sex happened, and it seems like you really disliked it. But you didn't say anything about the sex."

"Oh," you say, recollecting the evening. "The sex was fantastic."

"Then what are you complaining about?" the policeman says as he shuts the cruiser door.

"Why do you care if the sex was good?" you yell through the glass. But he ignores you. "That's a weird thing for a cop to ask a John who he just arrested, isn't it?"

Then again, some people hated the food, too.

☆☆☆☆☆ 5/2/2011

Eek! Methinks not

major attitude problems. the waitress thinks she is the shit for working at such an expensive restaurant. Listen girl, I am the shit cuz I can afford such an expensive restaurant. And the food was not good at all, served almost cold.

White Whine

Was this review ...? Useful ● (2)   Funny ● (1)   Cool ● (1)

Bookmark   Send to a Friend   Link to This Review   Add owner comment

---

Welcome to the Karma Cafe. No menu; you will get what you deserve.
Chicago, IL

Compliment
Send Message
Follow This Reviewer

☆☆☆☆☆ 11/27/2007

A particularly disgusting and bland little boite that I am forced to seek sustenance at during my self imposed professional (and thankfully temporary) exile in the hideous, no-reason-to-exist suburb of Schiller Park.

The food is odious. Bland. Shoddily presented. A bagel with processed cheese food substitute, microwaved eggs and faux ham has a faint taste of the food worker's horrible, cheap perfume. Revolting.

Breakfast orders consistently wrong. A request for BROWN mustard prompts a three minute discussion, no I don't want "honey mustard", I want REAL mustard.

Don't bother. Another reason to detest the suburbs.

White Whine

Was this review ...?   Useful ● (5)   Funny ● (3)   Cool ● (2)

Bookmark   Send to a Friend   Link to This Review   Flag this review

---

I left in tears

By teachlikestoeat on 7/16/2010

White Whine

Overall Rating: 4   Food: 5   Service: 1   Décor: 6   No, I would not go back!

This was the worst dining experience I have ever had in New York, or anywhere for that matter. They were seriously understaffed. The hostess ended up taking our order and bringing our drinks. We never had an actual server come to our table. We waited for long periods to get our drinks, and food. We had to ask the hostess for bread. Once we received our meal, we wanted to order wine, but no one ever came to take our order or even check on us. My husband finally had to get up and walk to the hostess stand to ask for a manager. When the manager finally came to the table, he was dismissive and told us their main focus was outdoor service in the summer and gave us the bill. I was so baffled by this rudeness after the horrible service on our anniversary, I burst into tears! He took the check away, rolling his eyes and stating, "Don't even worry about it". He walked away without any other words, not even an apology. I have never been more disappointed in the service industry. One of my favorite things about New York is the amazing restaurants and the service you get at these restaurants. I will pay top dollar for good service and a great meal, but I will NEVER return to Inside Park at St. Bart's and I suggest you, the reader, never do either.

Bed *Dread*

Going to bed is great. I wish I was doing it right now, but I have you goddamn people to entertain so I guess I'll stay awake. Beds have gotten increasingly more comfortable over the years—from rock, to dirt, to bag of hay, to spring coil, to bag of water, to memory foam—but one problem still plagues the First-World: Beds are just too damn big.

I know, it's incredible, but there are White Whiners out there who truly and honestly feel that their bed is just too big. This sounds crazy because, in general, we're always trying to get a bigger bed. From the cradle to the California king, we're always hunting for a bigger, plusher bed in which to lounge, love, and l'order a bunch of Thai food and watch TV. But White Whiners have achieved maximum bed space and now, blasphemously, they yearn to return to the days of . . . a twin? A double? Who knows what these crazy people are thinking.

To the rest of us, saying "my bed is too big" is right up there with saying any of the following: "This vacation was too free," "My spouse is too attractive," "My tax return is too large," "This Guinness World Record I have for Most Impressive Penis is too shiny," and "This book about White Whines I wrote sold too well and now I have too much money." In other words, things that we're all hoping to say at some point but probably never will. Especially that last one.

And the second to last one, too.

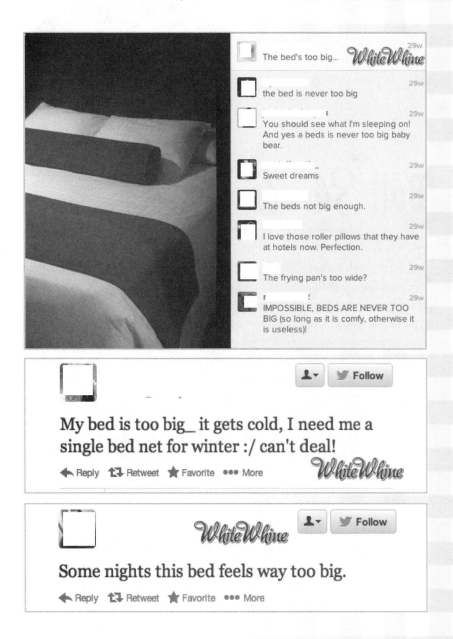

The bed's too big... *WhiteWhine* 29w

the bed is never too big 29w

You should see what I'm sleeping on! And yes a beds is never too big baby bear. 29w

Sweet dreams 29w

The beds not big enough. 29w

I love those roller pillows that they have at hotels now. Perfection. 29w

The frying pan's too wide? 29w

IMPOSSIBLE, BEDS ARE NEVER TOO BIG (so long as it is comfy, otherwise it is useless)! 29w

Follow

My bed is too big_ it gets cold, I need me a single bed net for winter :/ can't deal!

↩ Reply ↻ Retweet ★ Favorite ••• More   *WhiteWhine*

Follow *WhiteWhine*

Some nights this bed feels way too big.

↩ Reply ↻ Retweet ★ Favorite ••• More

85

Bull *Sheets*

It's not enough to have a bed, is it? There are a ton of accoutrements that one must purchase in order to make a bed more civilized. This seems strange considering what goes on in there (drooling, farting, sexing. In that order). You need a feather bed, a comforter, a fitted sheet, a top sheet, throw pillows, regular pillows, long cylindrical pillows (called "artificial men" I'm told), and a bunch of other ruffled, frilly things. And if you thought just having all that stuff was enough, you're wrong. The First-World sleepers not only demand all of these different bed dressings, but they also demand that they be made of the finest material. And if their bedding isn't up to snuff, the White Whines begin.

Thread count is the name of the game when it comes to sheets, and the higher the better. There's a bit of keeping up with the Joneses when it comes to thread count, too. Just a few years ago, 700 thread count was considered pretty luxurious. Now 700 thread count isn't fit for the homeless shelter, and unless you're working in the four-figure thread count zone, discerning First-World sleepers aren't interested.

And then of course there is Egyptian cotton, which is like regular cotton except more expensive. Made from the fleece of the pharaoh's personal flock of gilded sheep, this cotton is spun by a blind old oracle, and all who sleep under its silky warmth shall reap a good harvest and their first sons shall survive the plague. That's what Egyptian cotton should be for how much it costs, at least.

Moaning about thread count or cotton type is especially funny because these White Whiners can only truly appreciate the comfort and softness of these expensive luxuries when they are fast asleep. Yes, sound asleep . . . and probably dreaming of even higher thread counts and cottons from even more exotic locales.

Now *Lie in It*

I read somewhere that in the early medieval period, even kings and queens slept on simple piles of straw on the floor next to their whole families, their dogs, and their servants. Luckily, we've come a long way. Now we only let our dogs in our beds, not the dirty servants. Bedding itself has come a long way, too. Where, once, everyone slept on lousy straw mats, one can now choose to sleep on Intellicoil springs, Tempur-Pedic memory foam, or a glorified Ziploc bag full of probably-lethal chemicals called "ContourGel." In short, bedding is better. But with progress comes pain (at least according to a motivational poster I saw once of a guy climbing a rock). Some of the most luxurious sleepers, sadly, seem to be the most uncomfortable.

We've already discussed those who, having reached maximum bed size, long for a return to a smaller mattress. But they are a rare breed. Most nocturnal White Whiners long for a bigger bed. Put one of these people in a full bed and they'll beg for a queen. Give them a queen and they'll beg for a king. Give them a king and they'll beg for a California king. Give them a California king and they'll ask you to go to the shed and build them something even bigger, to be named later. If by some miracle they have found a bed that is large enough to accommodate their normal-size bodies, the next problem is usually with the dressing.

Some people find the number of things that go on a bed simply irritating, as if having a bunch of sheets, pillows, and blankets is somehow a bad thing. Still more White Whiners, though, take issue with what's inside. Feathers have a pointy end, and that is a major problem for those who choose to bed down on a fluffy feather-stuffed cloud every night. They toss and turn, but no matter which direction they angle their body a feather or two will always find a way to poke them. I like to think that the birds who were killed and defeathered to make the stuffing are reaching out from beyond the grave to torment the cause of their demise. But that was just a dream I had one night. On my tiny queen-size bed that's overflowing with unnecessary pillows. While being poked by goddamn feathers all night.

if one more of these damn goose feathers in my pillow stab me...I'm going to knock out the next bird I see

Like · Comment · about an hour ago via mobile · 👥

👍 3 people like this.

> ████████████████ dude i use to wake up with scratches on my face....
> about an hour ago · Like

> ██████████████████ I mean there comfy as shit but I'm constantly getting scratches too! THE FUCK...
> 59 minutes ago · Like

> ████████████████ i know and no matter what kind of pillow case u use it will still fuck u up
> 57 minutes ago · Like · 👍 1

> ██████████████ I have a down comforter to and it's always poking me wtf right
> 47 minutes ago · Like

Write a comment...

Maria   5h
I hate when feathers start poking through your pillow.
Collapse ← Reply ↻ Retweet ★ Favorite

3:23 AM - 19 Oct 12 · Details

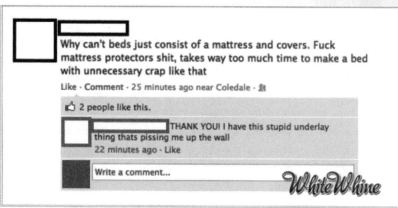

Why can't beds just consist of a mattress and covers. Fuck mattress protectors shit, takes way too much time to make a bed with unnecessary crap like that

Like · Comment · 25 minutes ago near Coledale · 👥

👍 2 people like this.

> THANK YOU! I have this stupid underlay thing thats pissing me up the wall
> 22 minutes ago · Like

Write a comment...

In the Closet

A closet must be an interesting notion for someone from a poorer part of the world. "So it's a room in your house?"

"Yes."

"That is only there to hold your clothes?"

"Yes."

"Because you have so many clothes that you needed to build a room in your house to hold them?"

"Yes, now can you please just take our picture? We'd like to see a few more sights before getting back on the cruise ship."

And while I'm sure we're all clutching our sides with laughter over that little sketch, it should be said that having a closet isn't really a luxury. I only bring them up here because certain First-Worlders have a major problem with their closets: They are just not big enough to hold all of their finery.

Expensive shoes are stacked up in easily toppled towers, shirts bend the bar under their massed weight, and dresses are squeezed so tightly together that the intense pressure might turn them into diamonds if just a little heat is added to the mix. None of this is the closet's fault, of course—I think we know who is to blame for having sixty pairs of shoes—but the closet will absorb all of the abuse. It's like gaining so much weight that your favorite chair snaps like a twig beneath you and, after being helped to your feet by a team of people and a few draft horses, you decide that the solution to that problem is buying stronger chairs, not losing weight. And that is a First-World solution to a First-World Problem.

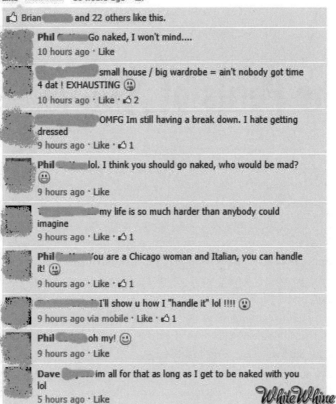

My life will never be anything but chaos until I have a house big enough to fit ALL of my clothes in it under one roof !!!! Until then I should be allowed to go around naked

Like · Comment · 10 hours ago ·

👍 Brian ____ and 22 others like this.

> Phil ____ Go naked, I won't mind....
> 10 hours ago · Like

> ____ small house / big wardrobe = ain't nobody got time 4 dat ! EXHAUSTING 😩
> 10 hours ago · Like · 👍 2

> ____ OMFG Im still having a break down. I hate getting dressed
> 9 hours ago · Like · 👍 1

> Phil ____ lol. I think you should go naked, who would be mad? 😃
> 9 hours ago · Like

> ____ my life is so much harder than anybody could imagine
> 9 hours ago · Like · 👍 1

> Phil ____ You are a Chicago woman and Italian, you can handle it! 😩
> 9 hours ago · Like · 👍 1

> ____ I'll show u how I "handle it" lol !!!! 😲
> 9 hours ago via mobile · Like · 👍 1

> Phil ____ oh my! 😊
> 9 hours ago · Like

> Dave ____ im all for that as long as I get to be naked with you lol
> 5 hours ago · Like

WhiteWhine

✕

Just got home and my shoe organizer fell. So annoying. Too many shoes and not enough room. Ikea here we come.

📱 30 minutes ago via iPhone · Like · Comment

👍 2 people like this.

> Brian ____ whitewhine.com
> 2 seconds ago · Like

WhiteWhine

Christian
Single ply toilet paper is bullshit... What is this a third world country?
8 minutes ago via Text Message · Like · Comment

Matthew likes this.

Nick #whitewhine
3 seconds ago · Like

White Whine

Write a comment...

The Perils of *Single Ply*

As a child, a great tome written by a sage philosopher once assured me that everybody poops. As I've grown I've found this to be true. Even the really pretty girls I went to high school with, I'm realizing. Yes, from the mightiest king to the lowliest servant, we all must get rid of yesterday's food. And while pooping may be universal, how comfortable the experience is varies greatly, especially when it comes to toilet paper. Just having access to a steady supply of toilet paper is a luxury in and of itself in many parts of the world (I've had friends travel to India and return with chilling tales of sponges on sticks). But to First-World White Whiners, not any toilet paper will do. I'm speaking of course about single ply toilet paper and the rage it summons by those unfortunates who are forced to use it.

It's a simple fact that some people just believe their asses deserve better than single ply. They've seen the Charmin bears wiping with sublime smiles plastered on their cartoon faces, delighting in the supple softness of a thick Charmin roll, and they want that for themselves every time they unload. On the occasion when their only option is military-issue single ply, these Whiners fly into a rage and alert the world via Twitter of the tragedy that has befallen their pampered asses.

Now of course we all love a comfy wipe with lotion-infused octo-ply paper, but I'm just hoping that when that kind of toilet paper isn't available, these White Whiners can still get the job done with single ply. If not, that's a much bigger problem.

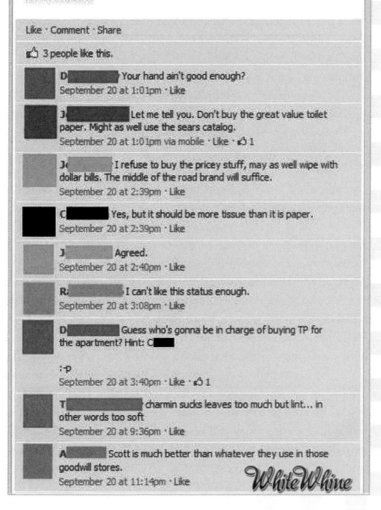

C___
Friday

Random thought: I just wanted to let you all know, there is NO EXCUSE for bad toilet paper.

If all you can afford is a 4-pack of Scott tissue, buy a 1 pack of Charmin! If all you can afford is a 1 pack of Scott Tissue, stand by the side of the road asking for spare change.

NO EXCUSES!

Like · Comment · Share

👍 3 people like this.

> **D___** Your hand ain't good enough?
> September 20 at 1:01pm · Like

> **J___** Let me tell you. Don't buy the great value toilet paper. Might as well use the sears catalog.
> September 20 at 1:01pm via mobile · Like · 👍 1

> **J___** I refuse to buy the pricey stuff, may as well wipe with dollar bills. The middle of the road brand will suffice.
> September 20 at 2:39pm · Like

> **C___** Yes, but it should be more tissue than it is paper.
> September 20 at 2:39pm · Like

> **J___** Agreed.
> September 20 at 2:40pm · Like

> **R___** I can't like this status enough.
> September 20 at 3:08pm · Like

> **D___** Guess who's gonna be in charge of buying TP for the apartment? Hint: C___
>
> :-p
> September 20 at 3:40pm · Like · 👍 1

> **T___** charmin sucks leaves too much but lint… in other words too soft
> September 20 at 9:36pm · Like

> **A___** Scott is much better than whatever they use in those goodwill stores.
> September 20 at 11:14pm · Like

WhiteWhine

93

Disappointing Gifts

Jesus's parents were probably among the first people to complain about a gift. "I love the gold but the frankincense and—what is this shit?—myrrh? For an infant?" Mary probably said after the Three Wise Men left the manger.

"Also," added Joseph, "who were those guys? We didn't know them, right? I think they just showed up. Weird."

Complaining about a gift is one of the most common White Whines. However, it's important to remember that because not all gifts are created equal, complaints about them are not created equal either. While someone fuming about a crappy $10 CVS gift card is slightly irritating, it's nothing next to someone who is fuming about the gross indignity of getting the wrong color BMW for their sixteenth birthday. The better the present, the more infuriating it is to realize you live in a world that doesn't execute people complaining about getting free cars for their birthday.

There is another variable to take into account when we decide how much we're going to hate one of these people, too: the depth of their anger. "Ugh, my mom got me an Android phone when I asked for an iPhone," is bad. But "I. Hate. My. Fucking. Parents! I'm going to kill myself with this stupid fucking Android phone so they'll never forgive themselves. I want to die but I want them to die first!" is much, much worse.

And much more fun for the rest of us! At the very least, we can take comfort in enjoying the fact that people like this will never ever be happy. Their life may hop from luxury to luxury, but for all of the temporal treasures they will never feel anything other than disappointment. That's probably why when Jesus grew up he tried to encourage people to find happiness internally: He was sick of hearing Mary and Joseph whine about "this idiot" who gave her divine son "myrrh or some bullshit" instead of a "gift that makes any fucking sense" for a baby. Like gold.

I fucking hate the car my parents got me.

Like · Comment · 10 minutes ago via mobile · 👤

👍 likes this.

Why don't you get yourself a car then
4 minutes ago · Like

Kids lose "bad mother" lawsuit. Can't take mom to court over bad birthday cards.

 by Piper Weiss, Shine Staff, on Tue Aug 30, 2011 10:40am PDT
4693 Comments | Post a Comment | Read More from This Author » | Report Abuse

f Share **33K** retweet **261** ✉ Email 🖨 Print

Open Question   Show me another »

Jake

So depressed?! My mom bought Chevy Orlando LTZ!?

Im 14 and a boy. Last month my mom Bought the best model with heated seats not leather though for 36k. But for 25k we could have bought my dream car a hummer h3 alpha with heated leather seats, LCD screen, sun roof, Bluetooth, tons of airbags, and a ton of other stuff. It's WAYYY better but my mom wouldn't buy it cuz she said its a gas guzzler. But who cares its the sexiest thing in the world and for -10k we could have got 4WD not FWD and way more accessories. Why is my mom blind to the truth. We've had it for 1 month.

2 minutes ago - 4 days left to answer.

It really makes me mad how selfish my parents can be. They told me a year ago that they're gonna save up for my sweet 16 this year, so I can have a party. But they, mainly my mom, decide to go a shopping spree, and they just spend a lot of money on stupid shit, then they come and tell me they "don't have enough money". Y'know, it's not like I've been planning this. Fuck you guys.

Like · Comment · 5 minutes ago near Dunedin · 👤

  and 14 others like this.

 Write a comment...

Pet Peeves

Ever since one of our ancestors—and let's be honest, probably a really, really stupid one—decided to steal a wolf cub and feed it, we've been smitten with our furry, fuzzy, cuddly prisoners. Pets brighten a home, provide endless hours of entertainment, and never ask for anything in return except some food, shelter, and a few toys. But pet ownership has its drawbacks, especially for White Whiners.

For starters, pets are animals (hopefully), which means they do animal things like pee and poop whenever they want and/or chew and eat whatever could possibly, maybe, sort of, be interpreted as food. Worse still, they don't care whether the object they're peeing on and/or eating is a toy or, say, a super expensive handbag that I JUST BOUGHT, GODDAMN IT! BAD! BAD DOG! Furthermore, pets, being animals, are not allowed into some human places, like stores. This is beyond frustrating for White Whiney pet owners because they view their little animals not as they are, but as tiny, furry people who should be granted the same rights and liberties as anyone else wearing a little frilly dress.

Plus, pets require constant grooming because the only part of their body they seem to keep clean on their own is their asshole. Whining about a bad groomer or a bad pet haircut is so clearly a First-World Problem that if someone in the Third World heard it, they would think it was a joke. "Ha! Paying someone to cut a dog's hair? That's funny," they would chuckle. "Now can you please help us dig this well so our village may have fresh water?"

Saddest of all pet-related White Whines are those from the pet deprived. I remember pining for a puppy as a little boy and being heartbroken every day that one did not arrive at my house. It's truly sad to want to own a pet but not be able to afford one. Right up until you read that the pet a person is pining for is not some lovable mutt, but rather an expensive, specific dog breed, or a pony. Then it becomes an almost blinding White Whine.

Anyone want a couple of cute ass cats? Can no longer afford to care for em. :(prefer they stay together, though!

Like · Comment · Get MyPad · about an hour ago via MyPad for iPad ·

WhiteWhine 18 comments

Ni

Livid. Milou and I got kicked out of Food Emporium, even though I was carrying her in my arms, AND she was wearing her adorable pink parka. Do these people not have souls?

2 hours ago · Like · Comment   *WhiteWhine*

49
92

San Francisco, CA

 7/3/2007

A store on Union Square that doesn't allow me to bring in my Chihuahua?! An outrage! And I was prepared to spend some money, too.

The door guy said no dogs allowed unless I brought him in in a bag. What if I had a large dog? they don't fit in bags. You can't discriminate between a large dog and a small dog. That's crazy and illegal. Plus, I don't put my dog in a bag unless I'm going on the bus, and that's because they make me.

Screw them, I'm taking my business elsewhere.

Listed in: Where I get my fix.

WhiteWhine

Was this review ...? Useful • (1)   Funny • (3)   Cool • (1)

Bookmark   Send to a Friend   Link to This Review   Add owner comment

---

Paula
33 seconds ago

Hate not having a pony to go and play with.. cant wait to get my new one :)

Like · Comment   *WhiteWhine*

Kaylee
worse day of my life...
my dog peed on my vera bradley backpack.

Like · Comment · 18 minutes ago near San Antonio, TX ·

9 people like this.

Write a comment...   *WhiteWhine*

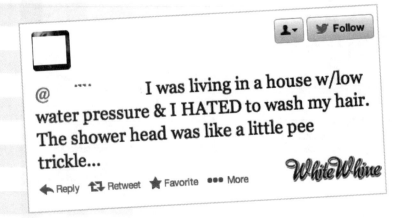

Under *Pressure*

If cleanliness is next to godliness, then consider the First-World a bunch of deities. There has never been a cleaner group of people since the ancient Romans had their bodies oiled up and then scraped by scantily clad bath boys. At the first sign of potential dirtiness, First-Worlders leap into action, scrub their hands with antibacterial soap, and then squeeze out a healthy dollop of Purell in order to obliterate whatever contagion may or may not have fouled their fingers. And though we have plenty of products that promise to kill 99.9 percent of germs—leaving 0.1 percent alive to tell the others what happened here, I guess—our primary means of erasing nature's stain is the shower. And White Whiners' primary complaint about their showers is that there's just not enough pressure.

Considering a good portion of the world still bathes in rivers, lakes, tubs, or not at all, having easy access to a shower is already a luxury. But a shower is just not luxurious enough for these White Whiners unless there is enough water pressure to not only blast away germs, dirt, and oil but also a few layers of skin. Anything less is met with a flood of White Whines about the painfully prolonged experience of trying to wash one's hair, clean one's skin, and/or relax one's mind in a low pressure shower. "It is," they claim, "like being peed on."

Which is also something wealthy Romans probably enjoyed.

Harried by Sperry

If White Whiners had a uniform, Sperrys would be the official footwear. Their stiff, blister-inducing backs are perfect for marching up to the Bloomingdale's customer service desk and demanding to know why they knowingly sold you the older model of All-Clad cookwear when they knew a newer model was coming out in a few months. The un-tie-able laces of these shoes give just the right amount of hold to walk from the practice tees to the clubhouse while muttering something about how the greenskeeper should really tuck in his shirt. And the rubber soles have the perfect amount of wet-weather grip to keep your footing on the deck of a pitching sailboat as you struggle to push a business rival to his death in the heaving waves. Yes, Sperry loafers have a long, storied history with White Whiners, making them at once the First-World's favorite shoe . . . and its favorite shoe to bitch about.

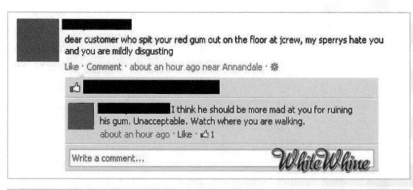

dear customer who spit your red gum out on the floor at jcrew, my sperrys hate you and you are mildly disgusting

Like · Comment · about an hour ago near Annandale · ❀

I think he should be more mad at you for ruining his gum. Unacceptable. Watch where you are walking.
about an hour ago · Like · 👍 1

Write a comment...

WhiteWhine

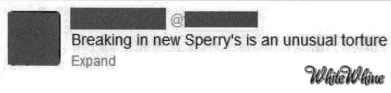

@

Breaking in new Sperry's is an unusual torture
Expand

WhiteWhine

French Cuffs

If you look at pictures of how respectable men dressed 200 or 300 years ago, it's quite a spectacle. There were wigs, frilly shirts, enormous overcoats, shiny buckle shoes, stockings, face powder, and a million other things that would make you double over with laughter if you saw someone wearing them today. At some point we wised up and got rid of the frills. These days, respectable men usually dress fairly simply: suit, shirt, tie, shoes (sans buckle). But one little vestige of that bygone era exists: the French cuff. And apparently, they're a huge pain in the ass.

But what is a French cuff? According to the White Whiners who choose to wear them, they're an "annoying" style of dress shirt that "sucks," and whose "stupid" cuffs are folded back on themselves and secured with "ugly ass" cuff links. It seems that they are impossible to find in one's size, impossible to do much of anything while wearing them, and impossible to keep clean. But they look good, right? Yes. No. Who knows?

All I know is that I once had a shirt with French cuffs. I wore it one time. My friends called me Captain Streeter the Fat Pirate. And that was the end of that.

Elliott
It's really hard to type in french cuffs
Like · Comment · 11 minutes ago · 🕮

> **Colleen** www.whitewhine.com
> 9 minutes ago · Like · 👍 1 person

> **David** You are the only person who would have a problem like this.
> 4 minutes ago · Like · 👍 1 person

WhiteWhine

Ahmad
I can never find French cuff in my size this sucks always have to custom tailor
Like · Comment · 49 minutes ago via mobile · 🕮

> **Tim** oh boo hoo... I wish I can wear somthing other then army gear....lol
> 48 minutes ago · Like

> **Ahmad** No it does suck man for work brotha just like you your working
> 43 minutes ago via mobile · Like

> **Jimand** white whine....
> a few seconds ago · Like

WhiteWhine

 I 🔽 **Follow**

staple your french cuffs

← Reply ⇄ Retweet ★ Favorite ••• More *WhiteWhine*

 🔽 **Follow**

Reaffirming my love/hate relationship with French cuffs.

← Reply ⇄ Retweet ★ Favorite ••• More *WhiteWhine*

I Don't *Wanna Work*

It's no secret that the American economy has been going through some growing pains this past decade. And by that I mean that it grew too big and then collapsed back in on itself, screwing over every sucker who bought into the American Dream. Whoops! Jobs are hard to come by these days, as many a twenty-eight-year-old living at home with their parents will confirm. But not everyone's dreams have been dashed. Somehow, a few people have managed to join the workforce. You might think that for these people steady employment is a good thing. But that's not entirely true. It seems that even in dire economic times, some people just really, really don't want to go to work.

Complaining about a job when millions of people are struggling to find work is clearly among the most obnoxious White Whines one could hear, especially if you happen to be one of those people struggling to find work. It's like suffering from the effects of a prolonged drought while reading tweets from someone in Seattle complaining about the horrible rainy weather. It's like being a disabled person in a wheelchair and hearing someone complain about how hard jogging is. It's like being an ugly, hopeless virgin and having Ryan Gosling seek you out to bitch about how all the beautiful women he's bedding aren't fulfilling him in any meaningful way.

What's particularly grating is that these White Whiners don't have a problem with the specifics of their jobs. They don't take issue with their mean-spirited boss, their monotonous tasks, or their unsafe working conditions. No, they take issue with the fact that they have to have a job at all. This may be good news for any unemployed person searching for work. Maybe these full time White Whiners will get their fill of this whole "working" thing one day and just quit. This would open up all kinds of employment opportunities for the millions of eager workers just waiting in the wings who will then, finally, have the chance to complain about having a job.

Okayyy I need a new job already. This is ridiculous.

Like · Comment

First day of work :)

Like · Comment

White Whine

Verizon 3G   11:32 AM   80%

Home   **Tweet**

Alison
White Whine

Now that I have a job I hate having a job

2/22/13, 11:32 AM

Home   Connect   Discover   Me

Music Snobs

Music is like wine. That was not meant to sound deep and profound (though clearly it does since I am an incredible wordsmith). Music is like wine in that pretty much everyone enjoys it. But among these people are a few self-appointed connoisseurs whose entire self-image is tied to the fact that nobody gets it quite like they do. The music snob, like the wine snob, is an evangelist for his passion, insisting that you listen to this song or that song while simultaneously declaring that you could never fully grasp its true beauty and importance because you lack the necessary education (i.e., reading Pitchfork every day for six months) to truly appreciate it.

What's particularly sad (and whiney) about music snobs is that their deep knowledge of music and its culture seems to prevent them from actually enjoying music. Why? For starters, you're there. That's right, you. A fellow fan perhaps, but of a far more inferior variety. And you simply don't know how to behave. I mean, singing along and dancing? At a concert? You should be ashamed of yourself. Music is meant to be contemplated and studied, not enjoyed. But you're not the only problem. Sometimes the venue isn't up to snuff or the music isn't sonically perfect. Both of those relatively minor issues can provoke long-winded, painfully irritating Facebook screeds.

These White Whiners sound like dethroned monarchs, longing for the good ol' days when a chamber orchestra could be summoned after dinner to privately entertain his highness and distinguished guests. Not only would they have the ability to really listen to the music, but if they didn't like the song, the venue, or the rest of the crowd, they could ban the song, burn the venue, and execute the crowd. Now that sounds like a concert!

I think what's most disappointing, is that there a good amount of people here in the US that don't want to educate themselves in the culture or history of electronic music. There's a good amount that aren't even going for the music, but to party with friends, get drunk, and do drugs. Imagine my frustration when I tell someone I like dubstep here in the USA, and I get the response "SKRILLEX RULES! DID YOU KNOW HE INVENTED DUBSTEP?"

Like · Comment · January 31 at 3:12pm near Boston · 🏢

👍 3 people like this.

> We're on the same page.
> January 31 at 3:18pm · Like

> Renata Roberta joe nice who?
> January 31 at 3:53pm · Like

> JoeNice is the President of Dubstep, his inauguration took place this weekend in Brooklyn @ Reconstrvct ft. Jack Sparrow, Lurka, Joe Nice, TrueNature
> January 31 at 3:56pm · Like

> skrillex obviously didnt invent dubstep but its kinda gay how everyone shits on him so much now cuz he became popular
> January 31 at 3:56pm · Like · 👍 1

> i had no idea there was an inauguration event haha how sweet
> January 31 at 3:59pm · Like

> It more his music and the vibe or should i say lack of vibe he brings... Just pilled up kids, girls and bros and their neon outfits, running around listening to robot noises claiming it to be 'dubstep, when they could care less about the actual music what so ever as long as they f**ked up'
> January 31 at 3:59pm · Like

> plus its annoying how many people claim to love BASS but can't even make the commitment to buy basic computer speakers with a sub, and just use macbook speakers....
> January 31 at 4:03pm · Like

White Whine

105

*Festi*FAIL

Music festivals have been a time-honored tradition in America since 1969 when, apparently, every single uncle in the country went to Woodstock. Festivals are different from concerts in that they're often multiday, outdoor affairs where one can see dozens of bands while taking drugs, instead of seeing just one band while taking drugs. But festivals aren't all fun and games (and drugs). Sometimes festivals go wrong in the most annoying ways. Just like drugs sometimes do, too.

Indiana State Fairgrounds Stage Collapse

Aug 14, 2011 9:46am
Length: 0:30

about an hour ago · Like · Comment · Share

This makes me angry. I'm supposed to see Maroon 5 there on Thursday ;(
about an hour ago · Like

well geez, what about the people who died under that stage!
about an hour ago · Unlike · 👍 1 person

Hey I feel for them... But I can't help but think that I J spent a shit ton of money on these tickets and it's only 4 days away! You can't build a stage that fast... Or can you? Idk.
about an hour ago · Like

you can build em in a few hours. i think you'll be alrite
about an hour ago · Like

I am sorry if this is your friend Christian...but...wow...Karen, how fucking selfish can you be?? That's seriously one of the most crass things that I have EVER heard uttered by a human being. No joke... And I've heard/ said some shit in my day. You literally just infuriated me. Maybe if the rest of the sane population of the world is lucky, a single stage light will fall during your stupid little Maroon 5 show, ending your life, and the dumb bitch standing next to you will start crying because your blood ruined her favorite shirt..
2 minutes ago · Like

WhiteWhine

Write a comment...

106

Wine *Whine*

Wine has long been the alcoholic drink of the upper crust, since to make it you need a certain type of rotten plant material that is far more difficult to cultivate than the rotten plant materials that create beer, vodka, rum, or whiskey. Because wine has such an elevated culture status, it's hard not to hear any complaint about wine as a White Whine.

It's as if wine Whiners are speaking a different language, some hybrid of French and English that only they can understand and that, they hope, will hide the truth: that what they're airing are First-World Problems. A person cannot drop a word like "sommelier" without coming off as a pretentious dork, just as someone cannot complain about "the shitter" without sounding like a hillbilly.

Even White Whinier than complaining about the wine is complaining about the wine-drinking lifestyle. Any issue with a home wine cellar, any problems about the order in which to serve the wines, any remorse over an expensive bottle of wine that has oxidized is, of course, a First-World Problem. Why? Because wine is a drink for the rich, beer is a drink for the normal, and water is a drink for the poor.

Unless it's FIJI Water. That's for the rich, too.

Why is someone writing about a 2006 Beaujolais in 2010? Isn't that a waste of bandwidth?

By **zin1953** on September 6, 2010 12:23 AM

David

Middleclass nightmare: Got the date wrong for a vintage port tasting and have now missed it. Appologies to both my valentines for my err. Totally heartbroken.

HOLLYWOOD

The Stars Whine Just Like Us

There was a time long ago when celebrities existed only in glossy magazines and on television and movie screens. Their words, their thoughts, their opinions, were only made public after the celebrity's lawyer, publicist, manager, and agent signed off on them. But then Twitter came along and all of a sudden celebrities had a way to directly communicate with their fans and the wider world. And what did they do with that tool? White Whine, of course.

About half the celebrity White Whines have to do with the celebrity not being treated like a celebrity. They have to fly Coach, they have to take out the garbage, their chauffeured car came super-duper late, and on and on. In other words, they're frustrated that they have to live like normal rich people instead of the hyper-rich people that they are. Some of these celebrity tweets could have been uttered by you or me, but the fact that a celebrity—someone who is better than us, remember—said them, makes them all the more Whiney.

The rest of the celebrity White Whines that come in are the complete opposite. I speak about the complaints that only the mega-rich could have. Most of these whines have something to do with a private jet. It seems that just like nonfamous million- and billionaires, celebrities can survey their extremely amazing lives and find faults all over the place. This is nothing new, of course. But thanks to Twitter, now we can all know exactly what minor hiccup in their otherwise blessed lives is giving them trouble.

@LilTunechi
Lil Wayne WEEZY F ✔

10 hour flight to Hawaii...sh!t!! I thought this thing was kalled a private JET! Geez Louise,dam Sam,and f#ck Chuck. This is that bullshhhhh

35 minutes ago via Twitter for iPhone

☆ Favorite   ⇄ Retweet   ↩ Reply

You know the worst part of buying a new golf club?? Having to wait til the next time you go golfing to use it! Ugh...

3:39 PM Apr 2nd via web
Retweeted by 3 people

frankiemuniz
Frankie Muniz

Perry Farrell
Last night we all took a private jet to Ottawa. The jet was run down inside. The crew's costumes needed a wash. One pilot spread himself out on the couch. I was confused. I thought flying a private jet, I'd be in the lap of luxury; but under the scrutinies of commercial flight. Not So. They are outsourced by individual charter companies.. Sketchy, in the sky...

All *Hopped Up*

Imagine someone who must have only the finest, most artisanal dental floss. They shun major-label dental floss, like GUM, and only use hand-spun, small batch dental floss from local manufacturers that costs five times as much, even though both flosses do the same thing. That would be weird, right? But that is the mentality of the modern day beer snob. Although the craft beer movement has been great for beer drinkers everywhere, it has created a sour by-product—no, not malt liquor—beer snobs who scoff at anything but the finest brews.

These poor White Whiners are just looking for a craft brewed, barrel aged, triple hopped, India pale ale. But what do they find instead? Disgusting domestic beer that doesn't even have its own special kind of glass. And while there are plenty of people who will loudly complain if no fancy beer is available, some Whiners take it a step into the surreal. I have hard evidence that there is at least one beer snob who refuses to drink beers "out of season." (Do certain types of alcohol work better in the fall?) That would really make grandpa laugh.

And as ridiculous as getting upset over beer may seem, it's hard not to jump on the microbrew bandwagon. So, if you find yourself sneering at any beer that costs less than $12 a bottle or is made in a factory, try this: force yourself to drink one. Then force yourself to drink two or three more. And then, like magic, you won't care whether you're drinking some pee-scented macrobrew or Uncle Felchman's Small Batch Belgian Abbey Oak Ale. The magic of alcohol!

R
Glad to be in the states where deciding what to beer to buy actually takes effort instead of the 2 choices you have in Thailand.

December 23, 2010 at 1:22pm · Like · Comment

 J   I couldn't do it, man.
December 23, 2010 at 1:31pm · Like

White Whine

C
tonight i wore a classic white and pink striped ralph lauren button down to work at the liquor store. someone tried telling me "they love" tommy hilfiger. i then told him i was wearing ralph lauren. his reply. . . 'same thing" i am pretty sure he would have been offended too if i told him to enjoy his natie stones

White Whine

I refuse to drink any fall beers before September... so please stop advertising them, I don't need this kind of stress right now.

15 minutes ago · Like · Comment

👍   and 2 others like this.

snob
11 minutes ago · Like

Your life must be incredibly difficult.
about a minute ago · Like

White Whine

Um, I Ordered a *Complicated Coffee,* So . . .

Everyone remembers the days when you could stroll into a joint and order a plain ol' cup of joe. The kid would ask, "cream and sugar?" and you'd say, "Nah, kid. Black." Then you'd light a cigarette and read the newspaper. Those were the days, apparently. These days ordering coffee is a complicated process that involves no less than 2,000 ingredients and preparation techniques. This has allowed for an endless array of customizable caffeinated beverages, thus ensuring that every single patron can get exactly the drink he or she wants. It also ensures that people are going to get their panties severely twisted when they don't get exactly. What. They. Ordered!

Any sort of milk, other than what they ordered, is a frequent problem. To be fair, it's actually fairly awful when, say, a soy milk drinker accidentally gets skim milk put in his or her beverage. If this person consumes the skim milk, his or her body reacts to the foreign substance by creating a certain type of antibody. This antibody attacks the skim milk, but the side effect is that it also causes the sufferer to go on Facebook and call the barista a dumbass bitch.

But so much more than milk can go wrong. The temperature can be off by a whopping three or four degrees. Whipped cream can be added or withheld, as can cinnamon, nutmeg, and a thousand other spices that people in centuries past used to die trying to find—and which we now dump on top of coffee foam because it looks nice. Worst of all, the idiot barista could make a venti caramel macchiato plus whip with three pumps instead of two! Can you imagine?! Having a drink with three pumps instead of two? I shudder to think . . .

And it's only going to get worse from here. First-Worlders have a taste for sugary, caffeinated drinks now, and it's not going away. The Whiners will drink more, refining their palates, creating ever more specific drink demands, and getting whinier and whinier when each and every drink doesn't come out perfect every single time. All that sugar and all that caffeine are like putting gasoline on the fire. Or sugar and caffeine into the White Whiner.

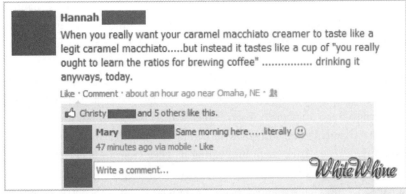

*Cilantr*OH NO

Cilantro is perhaps the most polarizing of leaves. For those who can tolerate its herbal spiciness there is simply nothing better. They will—and do—sprinkle it on everything. I know this because my wife is one of those people, so I've found little shards of cilantro in everything from eggs to steak. But for those who fail to appreciate its bite, nothing could be worse than finding cilantro on their plate. Literally nothing. Based on the tone of their complaints, you'd think they'd prefer to find a rat's raw eyeball in their torta or a full human toenail in their pasta over a single leaf of cilantro.

What makes them so Whiney is that their anger is based on the entirely flawed premise that everyone else in the world has the same palate they do. So the discovery of cilantro is never met with "I forgot to tell the waiter to hold the cilantro!" and instead with complete and utter shock that anyone would dare try to trick them into eating it. They seem to believe that chefs are playing a prank on them and include cilantro simply to cause them pain. What separates cilantro haters from diners who dislike other flavors is that the latter will still eat their food. I don't love black olives, but if I happen to find an olive in a seven-layer dip, I'll do my best to pick around it and still eat—or, more accurately, engulf—the dip. Anti-cilantroists will simply refuse to eat their food because, they claim, it is now inedible. "UGH! There's CILANTRO in this taco! Now I can't eat it!" they moan, as if a preference and an allergy are the same thing. If you can think of a better First-World Problem than not eating food because of one tiny ingredient—when Third-World food is often just one tiny ingredient—by all means let me know.

My father has celiac disease, meaning that he cannot eat gluten. When he goes out to eat, he makes a point to relay this fact to the waiter, often to an annoyingly thorough degree. While ordering dinner, it's not unusual for him to remind the waiter, up to ten times, that he cannot consume gluten. He will then proceed to interrogate the waiter about whether or not the unsweetened

114

iced tea is made with flour (Hint: it's not). He does all of this to ensure that the waiter will be vigilant with the kitchen staff so as to ensure that no gluten makes it onto his plate. This is how anti-cilantroists should conduct themselves. They must recognize that they are the ones being annoying, not the chef who chooses to use an interesting ingredient, and adjust their ordering preference to accommodate that reality.

But they won't. Maybe we should just go back to calling it coriander and start fresh.

Vengeful *Vegans*

Scientists believe that the reason humans became masters of the world was that we started to eat meat. The infusion of extra protein into our monkey bodies allowed our brains to grow, which in turn allowed us to form complex thoughts like, "Damn, meat is awesome," "Where and how can I get more of this meat," and "If I get really good at catching meat, maybe all the women in the group will want to have sex with me." It's surprising then that even though meat has allowed us to become brilliant masters of the world, there are some among us who decide to forgo all animal meat and animal-based products. These people are known as vegans, and though they may swear off everything delicious on God's green earth, they do not hold back when it comes time for a White Whine.

You see, being a vegan is a (self-inflicted) struggle. Most humans enjoy animal products for the simple reason that they are damn delicious. For this reason, most foods contain a little bit of animal. This is a problem for the vegan, and his solution is to loudly complain about it to anyone standing within earshot. All of this shouting has not, so far, resulted in the complete elimination of animal products from restaurants and grocery stores. But it has managed to mark vegans out as some of our society's most annoying people.

But the biggest problem with being a vegan is the cost. Society has decided that if someone doesn't want to play by the rules and eat the animals it has gone to the trouble of raising and killing, then those people are going to pay a premium for going against the grain. Or with the grain, I guess. Therefore, it's not difficult to find vegans who not only complain about the lack of vegan options but also the cost of the options that are available. It's a bit like if you or I decided that we were going to wear shoes on our hands instead of our feet, and then we went around moaning to anyone who would listen about how there only a few places that even have hand-shoes, and when you can find them, they cost an arm and a leg!

It almost makes you wonder why anyone would choose to be a vegan, what with the difficulty of finding food and the cost of the food that is available. And then you remember things like jogging, nipple piercing, and boxing, and you remember that some people just love to do things that suck.

August 5

With the exception of Pho Tre Bien, Trattoria Bella Sera, and Tom's, I am finding it increasingly difficult to dine in local restaurants with quality vegan morsels that can surpass (let alone meet) the caliber of my own creations. Considering my level of cooking experience—neophyte at best—and the offerings of local Gastronomy, El Paso's dining establishments are, in general, considerably lacking in quality vegan accommodations and cuisine.

Like · Comment

4 people like this.

View all 21 comments

In other words El Pasos vegan food is aight I can do it better. You're welcome everyone.
August 5 at 2:09pm via mobile · Like · 1

Key points: 1) There are some establishments with great vegan offerings; however, these establishments are thylacine in nature. 2) With respect to quality, what I can make tends to exceed the vegan morsels offered by most establishments; this should not be the case considering that I am considerably green in terms of culinary experience.
August 5 at 2:33pm · Like

you sould show me some dishes sometime!
August 5 at 3:21pm · Like

thylacine as in the marsupial?
August 5 at 8:47pm · Like · 2

Have you tried, that new steakhouse on the far east? Its been established vegan because all the cows apparently signed consent forms for consumption. Delicious!
August 5 at 8:59pm via mobile · Like · 1

Just like the rare sightings of the aforementioned marsupial, vegan eateries and delicious vegan offerings are either seldom seen or completely nonexistent in El Paso.
August 5 at 11:04pm · Like

White Whine

117

The Everyday *Gourmand*

Thanks to a surplus of disposable income and the spread of *Top Chef*–style programming, everybody alive in the United States today knows what an "amuse bouche" is. We can now rattle off hundreds of words and phrases that up until a decade ago were only understood by a handful of gourmet chefs. Indeed, fine dining has become a commodity in America and, as a result, a select group of amateur gourmands has coalesced around one aim: to criticize and complain about any and all food ever served or bought at a store. So not only are we lucky enough to be living in a country that is absolutely stuffed with food, but we're so well off that if that food isn't up to snuff, we can—and almost always will—complain about it!

Grocery stores are berated for running out of some exotic Indian grain or stocking the "wrong" kind of seedless grapes. Produce is criticized for being too small, too big, too bitter, or too sweet. Fine dining restaurants are subjected to some of the worst criticism for failing to deliver a flawless meal every single time. Even crazier is when the not-fine dining restaurants—of the Subway-McDonald's variety—are given no slack for their food. There is something borderline insane about people who hold a meal at McDonald's to the same standard they would hold a restaurant like Per Se. And yet, here we are.

And while I can understand how people expect the best out of every meal— even a meal at McDonald's, which is little more than poison masquerading as fast food—the one type of gourmet White Whiner I have no sympathy for is the linguistically accurate foodie. Like Henry Higgins, these foodies are obsessed with pronouncing every foreign food, ingredient, and preparation in its linguistically true, native form. If you can complain about an avocado pit being too big, I'm not going to ride you too hard; but if you insist on pronouncing the word avocado "like the Aztecs would," it will take every ounce of my will to not bean you in the eye with the "ayyvo-kaydu" pit.

Julie
I hate it when people pronounce "Venti" "Ven-Tay" at Starbucks. It seriously annoys the crap out of me. I probably couldn't work there for that reason.
1 hour ago via BlackBerry

WhiteWhine

👍 2 people like this.

I pronounce it "large". ;)
1 hour ago · Like · 👍 2

OK everyone:

PANINI = is ALREADY PLURAL

If you want to add an 's' like an anglo, at least use panino.

STOP LANGUAGE REDUNDANCY!

/publicserviceannouncement
Like · Comment · Share · 2 hours ago · 🌐
👍 8 people like this.
🗨 View all 15 comments

WhiteWhine

When faced w a need for mayonnaise I consulted Modernist Cuisine AND as long as you have Xanthan gum and a sous vide machine (I do) and the ability to whisk until your arm falls off the result is the best mayo I've ever had. And I don't like mayonnaise.

WhiteWhine

jo
It is impossible to make a good black tea at 10500 ft because water boils at 194F. #lame
11 Aug

WhiteWhine

I wish I was more enthused about this pomegranate
7 minutes ago

WhiteWhine

Started making my Maple Hemp Granola, then I realised I have no more maple syrup. Now I'll be stuck with Brown Rice Syrup/Agave-Hemp granola ughhh
Like · Comment · 3 hours ago · 🌋
👍 7 people like this.

WhiteWhine

Keurig:
Changing the Way We Complain about Coffee

Certain products come into the First-World and really shake things up. Skis changed the way First-Worlders complain about winter vacations. iPhones changed the way First-Worlders complain about technology. And now Keurig coffee machines are changing the way White Whiners complain about their coffee.

Gone are the days when brick and mortar coffee shops like Starbucks and Dunkin' Donuts were the only places to quietly seethe when your frappe isn't up to snuff. Now almost anyone can complain about coffee in the comfort of their own home thanks to this revolutionary system that White Whiners everywhere are calling "Shitty" and "I miss the old coffee machine." All you need to do is buy a Keurig machine (which is not a Nazi torture device) and some K-Cups (which are not exceptionally large breasts), and you'll be making coffee you hate in no time!

Of course, not everyone hates the Keurig Revolution (which is not a Nazi-endorsed racial uprising in Latin America). Some people love their Keurig. Like, a lot. Like, to the point where they will allow nothing to stand between them and their beloved, wheezing, gurgling coffee machine. Love it or hate it, complaining about a Keurig is a certified fair trade White Whine.

Mark my words: if you use a Kuerig maker in your office it will eventually fail you. Especially if you have hard water. Home use machine aren't meant to be used by a dozen caffeine addicts day in and day out. Then you won't have coffee. And you will be angry. And write rants on facebook.

Like · Comment · about an hour ago ·

likes this.

oohh nooo!! the worst thing that could happen to a mom happened to me....my KEURIG is BROKEN!!!!

White Whine

T

My boss replaced our Keurig with this piece of shit? WTF? Guess I'm going to Starbucks from now on.

White Whine

Steven
20 hours ago near Olive Branch · ✕

Wendy bought me a Keurig k-cup coffee machine, thank you. For someone who likes coffee it serves really bad coffee. Coffee comes out tasting and smelling like a cheap heating element. This was never going to replace my french press. So venturing to something shiny does not necessarily means good.

Like · Comment · Unfollow Post

👍 Lisa [redacted] likes this.

Will [redacted] Sounds delicious!
20 hours ago via mobile · Like

Smith Sounds like you got a new Whine Press.
20 hours ago · Like · 👍 1

White Whine

Trouble in the *Water*

Water makes up something like 70 percent of the human body, which explains why we leak so much in the form of pee, sweat, tears, and blood. We cannot live without it, but a good number of us seem to be prepared to do just that if a particular brand or style of water is not available. There are two tiers of water Whiners I've come across since I started the White Whine website: those who prefer bottled to tap and those who prefer one bottle to another. But don't worry, both are going to get made fun of here!

It's worth remembering that free-flowing water delivered into our homes and businesses is easily one of the greatest accomplishments of modern society. The Romans are remembered as one of antiquity's great civilizations, as much for their network of aqueducts, fountains, and baths as they are for their kick-ass army and tasteful orgies. The loss of running water following the collapse of the Roman Empire was one of history's great leaps backward, and for hundreds of years thirsty people had no choice but to go out and get their own water. This is essentially what our first group of water Whiners chooses to do in spite of the modern world's remastery of tap water (we're still sadly way, way behind on the orgy front).

There are certain things worth paying for in this world: a good bed, a quality skydiving instructor, and this book. But water is probably not one of them, unless you happen to be vacationing in the tropics or have signed over your land to a natural gas fracking company. Most of us will buy a bottle or two from time to time, but there's a big difference between that and only drinking bottled water. These people are committing to a lifestyle that costs infinitely more and produces the same results. It'd be like paying for AOL to go online. And yet, there are millions of them out there who do just that. Millions of people whine about how the tap water tastes and, more annoyingly, how drinking tap water makes them feel poor. We're not winning any friends in Africa with tweets like these, I can tell you that much.

Even more confusing are those among us who not only shun free tap water in preference to bottled water but also declare themselves brand loyal to a specific type of bottled water. The ingredients in water are as follows: 1. Water. So, if there is a difference in taste between a bottle of Aquafina and a bottle of Dasani, it's a difference in taste between the plastics used to manufacture the bottles. Some prefer the more expensive plastic used in FIJI Water, while more common folk will settle for the plastic used in Poland Spring or Deer Park. And even if certain waters do have a superior taste, since when is that a good thing? Clean water isn't supposed to taste like anything, just like good vodka isn't supposed to taste like anything (except fire). Water tasting like anything seems like it should raise a red flag, not a thumb.

Next time you encounter a water Whiner of either stripe, try out this fun experiment. First, go out and buy a bottle of expensive water like smart water or FIJI. Then dump out the bottle, fill it with tap water from your house, and put it in the fridge. The next time they come over, offer them the water bottle and make a show of opening it (so they don't realize it's already been opened). And then dump it on their head.

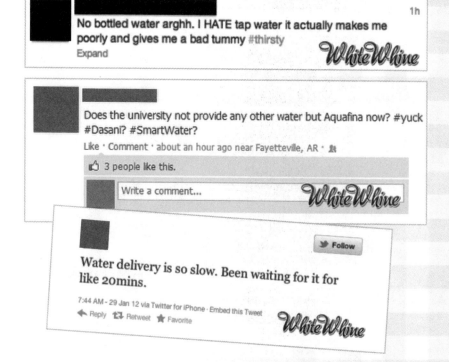

123

I Ate *Too Much*

"I ate too much." In my family, this is a frequently uttered First-World Problem. Yes, it is a common White Whine, but it may also be one of the most obnoxious if, say, you are from a household where getting enough food for everyone is a problem. Furthermore, having too much food isn't really a problem—unless it's starting to attract bears and other wildlife.

Even the idea of having "too much food" is a little absurd. It's up there with "I'm too respected," "I'm too smart," and "I'm too funny." I don't want to say these things can't be a problem; it's just that they're not the kind of problem anyone is going to feel bad about. These are good problems. So is having too much food. And when you complain about a good problem, that, my friend, is White Whining.

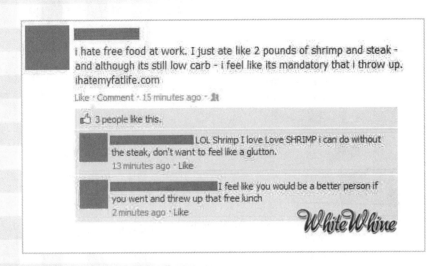

i hate free food at work. I just ate like 2 pounds of shrimp and steak - and although its still low carb - i feel like its mandatory that i throw up. ihatemyfatlife.com

Like · Comment · 15 minutes ago ·

3 people like this.

LOL Shrimp I love Love SHRIMP i can do without the steak, don't want to feel like a glutton.
13 minutes ago · Like

I feel like you would be a better person if you went and threw up that free lunch
2 minutes ago · Like

WhiteWhine

124

Golf Grumbling

Golf was invented in Medieval Scotland during the three weeks when they weren't being massacred by the English. Since then, golf has grown to become the First-World's favorite summertime sport. Like so many sports, golf requires an extreme amount of expensive gear, time, and space. But unlike most others, the "sport" of golf demands almost no physical effort. Given the fact that golf is almost always played in nice weather during the summer, and that a sneeze requires more effort than playing eighteen holes, any complaint about golf is an automatic White Whine.

Most golfers are pretty content just to be out there playing, even if the course is ragged and some asshole isn't replacing his divots. It's only when golfers can't play that the White Whines start teeing off.

And if you think that complaining about the inability to do something sounds more Third-Worldy than First-Worldy, imagine vocalizing this complaint to someone who had never heard of golf: "Ugh, I wish I could spend six hours walking around a giant grass park, in the sunshine, with my friends, trying to hit a little ball into a hole with metal sticks that cost me $2,400 and then go to a mansion in the park and get drunk on alcohol and talk about our best and worst hits we made with those metal clubs."

Exactly.

Mike ▇▇▇▇ Unbelievable. First time it has rained in weeks and it's the day of my golf sand lesson.

6 hours ago via Facebook for iPhone · Comment · Like *White Whine*

Training,
Complaining at the Gym

As someone who has worked out occasionally, I can tell you that working out is the absolute worst. You're taking a perfectly fine body and subjecting it to painful tests of strength, all so that you will hopefully tear your muscle fiber and it will grow back bigger. Unfortunately, every single doctor on the planet seems to have gotten together and decided to prank humanity by insisting that this painful daily ritual is necessary to one's health. So we all work out, and most of us complain about it. But complaining that your body is in physical pain because you've just picked up a heavy piece of metal fifty times isn't a White Whine. No, it takes a little bit of extra luxury to create a fitness White Whine. And luckily I know just where to find that luxury: the gym.

Just having a gym in which to blast your glutes, shred your pecs, and, most important, stare at yourself in the mirror for ten minutes is a bit of a luxury. However, for some people, it's not enough. Without even getting into specifics, these people White Whine because they have to share their gym with other people. Other people! At their gym! What's this world coming to?

But where White Whiners go above and beyond is the attacks they make on the various luxuries and amenities found at their gyms.

But where can one find luxury at the gym? Aren't gyms supposed to be sweaty, dank, dark rooms full of shady Russians named Alexei who offer to help "supplement your pump, my friend" with some off-brand cattle hormones? Yeah, I thought so, too. But it seems that, in reality, modern gyms put exercising a few steps behind a well-staffed smoothie station. In other words, luxuries to White Whine about are readily available in most gyms without having to look too hard. Personal trainers roam the gym like hyenas, part of the same pack but each only looking out for himself. Diversions—magazines, TVs, etc.—have been wedged into every available surface in an

126

effort to trick people into thinking they're actually having fun. Freelance masseuses camp out by their tables and try to get paid $75 to dig their elbows into peoples' backs. Gyms are so luxurious now that it's almost impossible to be a member of one and not turn into a White Whiner.

Oh, and don't worry, Alexei is still there selling cattle hormones in the locker room. Only now you have to buy him a Blueberry Blast Smoothie before he'll do business with you.

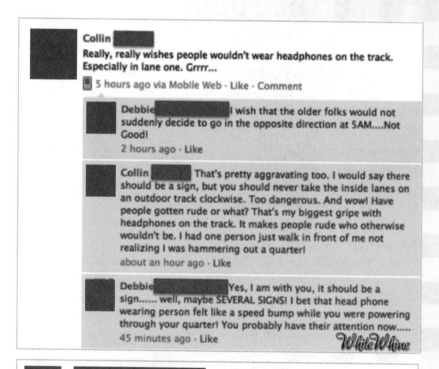

Collin ▓▓▓▓
Really, really wishes people wouldn't wear headphones on the track. Especially in lane one. Grrrr...
5 hours ago via Mobile Web · Like · Comment

> **Debbie** ▓▓▓▓ I wish that the older folks would not suddenly decide to go in the opposite direction at 5AM....Not Good!
> 2 hours ago · Like

> **Collin** ▓▓▓▓ That's pretty aggravating too. I would say there should be a sign, but you should never take the inside lanes on an outdoor track clockwise. Too dangerous. And wow! Have people gotten rude or what? That's my biggest gripe with headphones on the track. It makes people rude who otherwise wouldn't be. I had one person just walk in front of me not realizing I was hammering out a quarter!
> about an hour ago · Like

> **Debbie** ▓▓▓▓ Yes, I am with you, it should be a sign...... well, maybe SEVERAL SIGNS! I bet that head phone wearing person felt like a speed bump while you were powering through your quarter! You probably have their attention now.....
> 45 minutes ago · Like

Really wish people would stop stealing all the chick magazines from the gym. Now I'm stuck reading The Economist for the next hour. Awesome.

Like · Comment · Share ▓▓ on Twitter · 22 minutes ago via Twitter · ▓

👍 2 people like this.

Nothing Fits
My Perfect Body

Bodies have a funny way of not doing what you want them to do. For instance, try as I might, I cannot convince my body to become 6' 3" and 185 pounds of lean muscle. I have to settle for 6' 1" and 225 pounds of what I like to call the American Mix of too much bone, too much muscle, and way too much fat. I'm not alone, either. A full 100 percent of people alive today are not satisfied with their bodies—thanks, advertising! But interestingly, the only group to really loudly complain about it are those among us who really should be happy with the skin they're in.

Women who wear size 0 or 00—which I'm told is an enviable size to wear—are having a hard time finding clothes that fit. And wouldn't you know it, they're not afraid to let the whole world know about their troubles. Complaints range from things just "not fitting right" to "having to shop in the kids' section." Both are horrible tragedies that nobody should have to endure. These kinds of complaints are doubly frustrating simply because (1) the Whiner wants you to feel bad for them for being thin while, at the same time, (2) letting everyone know just how thin they are. It would be like hearing someone say, "UGH! I can't find a safe big enough to hold all my gold bullion!"

What's even more frustrating, especially to a larger person like me, is the fact that I know all of these bone bags will outlive me. I'll be in the ground early from some combination of diabetes, heart disease, and, hopefully, a fatal choking incident during a cheeseburger eating contest, while they're still walking the earth, moaning about their enviable forms.

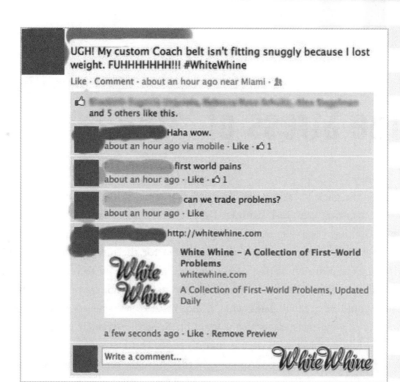

UGH! My custom Coach belt isn't fitting snuggly because I lost weight. FUHHHHHHH!!! #WhiteWhine

Like · Comment · about an hour ago near Miami · 🐜

👍 ▬▬▬▬▬▬▬▬▬▬▬▬▬▬
and 5 others like this.

▬▬▬▬▬▬▬▬ Haha wow.
about an hour ago via mobile · Like · 👍 1

▬▬▬▬▬▬▬▬▬ first world pains
about an hour ago · Like · 👍 1

▬▬▬▬▬▬▬▬▬ can we trade problems?
about an hour ago · Like

▬▬▬▬▬▬▬▬▬ http://whitewhine.com

White Whine – A Collection of First-World Problems
whitewhine.com
A Collection of First-World Problems, Updated Daily

a few seconds ago · Like · Remove Preview

Write a comment...

4 hours ago near ▬▬▬▬▬ ia Mobile 🐜

Not being able to buy pretty dresses because the smallest size is too big suuuuuuuucks :'(

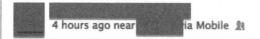

why is it when ever I want to online shop my size is never available. Is skinny tall people not aloud to exist. FML. im jst going to constantly eat my candy and wait for the pounds to pack on so I can buy normal clothes.

Like · Comment · 11 minutes ago near ▬▬▬▬▬ · 🐜

Mary ▬▬▬
My fave jeans are too big. They are only size 0. Fml

Like · Comment · 24 minutes ago via mobile · 🐜

 Crystal ▬▬▬ wish has even half my size
8 minutes ago via mobile · Like

The Stress of *Yoga*

Yoga is the ancient eastern art of sitting still while still telling everyone that you're working out. Just kidding; I don't really know what yoga is. But I do know that yoga is extremely popular with women for its many spiritual and physical benefits; and popular with men for the many female physical attributes that are on display at yoga class. Yoga is meant to relax the body, increase circulation, and, most of all, offer its practitioners peace of mind. That would be great if that's what it did. Instead, it seems to make a good number of yoga-meisters (which is what I call them) extremely uptight.

The first problem with yoga is that it's hard. This fact seems to catch most White Whiners by surprise. Apparently they thought that twisting up into a pretzel shape and balancing on one hand for ten minutes would be a relatively easy trick to perform. Of course, yoga is not hard when compared to, say, any other sport. But I'll let the yoga-meisters off easy in my book because I've thrown the word "hard" around a lot. According to me, the following things are "hard": drawing Batman, untying my shoe, most video games, and choosing what I want at a Thai restaurant.

The yoga Whiners that really crack me up are the ones for whom yoga is one of the most stressful parts of their day. These people really want to partake in the serenity that is standing on one leg while pointing at the ceiling but, goddamn, the drive there is stressful, making it on time is stressful, and doing the moves properly is stressful. This of course defeats the entire purpose of yoga. It's like being prescribed antidepressants but then getting super depressed because you need to be on antidepressants. It's a vicious cycle that nobody wins. Except us, the readers of this book, who get to laugh at the people who somehow manage to be uptight about yoga.

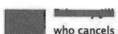
who cancels yoga??? I mean I know it's a snow storm and all but I
need my mediation don't these people know I have a test on
Monday! rawrrrrrr

Like · Comment · 6 minutes ago near ■■■■ · ⚙

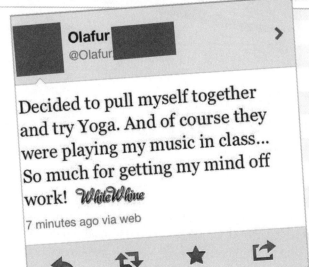

Olafur
@Olafur

Decided to pull myself together
and try Yoga. And of course they
were playing my music in class...
So much for getting my mind off
work!

7 minutes ago via web

A wasteful day makes me feel sick. Just
spent an hour and a half in traffic to go to
yoga and I was too late. FU*K

← Reply ↻ Retweet ★ Favorite ••• More

My yoga class stresses me out

← Reply ↻ Retweet ★ Favorite ••• More

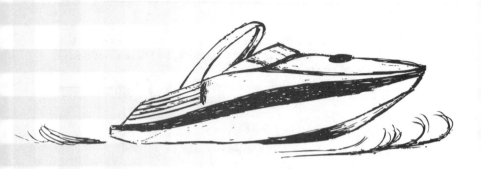

Boat *Gloating*

Every boat-owning uncle in these United States claims to have originated the phrase, "The best two days of owning a boat are the day you buy it and the day you sell it." They're all liars. My Uncle Eddie made up that line, but that's beside the point. Any complaint about a boat is an automatic White Whine, because it implies that the Whiner owns—or at least regularly enjoys—a boat.

Based on the number of seemingly dissatisfied boat owners in the country, it appears that owning a boat is pure torture; as if Hades himself pioneered the concept of boats solely to keep people in a perpetual state of misery. Slip fees are "outrageous," winterizing a boat is "agonizing," and it takes millions to keep up with the Joneses at the marina. But we know better, don't we? We've all seen music videos. Clearly, 90 percent of boat ownership is having a wonderful time with beautiful people and only 10 percent is dealing with the hassle . . . or paying other people to deal with the hassle.

My hunch is that boat owners need to cover for the fact that their lives are significantly better than the rest of the population's. So, they complain about owning a boat in a misguided attempt to make us think, "Oh, poor Mike and that boat of his. Is there no end to his troubles?" And they would get away with it, too, if it weren't for the fact that every boat owner, no matter how often he complains, cannot help himself from posting pictures on Facebook of just how much more fun he's having than everyone else out on the sea.

Bra████

Think your having a bad day, try putting 500 in gas in your boat

Mobile Uploads

10 hours ago via Android · Like · Comment · Share

👍 Tony Adams likes this.

> ████████ Get a smaller tank
> 10 hours ago · Like

> ████████ Damn you must wanna tube bad.
> 10 hours ago · Like

> ████████ you should caulk a Prius shut so it will
> float....better gas mileage
> 10 hours ago · Like   ✕

> ████████ at least you got a boat!
> 10 hours ago · Like

> Bra██ All the above answers are good ones. Haha
> 10 hours ago · Like

> ████████ U must have filled up on the water
> 9 hours ago · Like

> Bra██ Bryan, that's an awesome idea
> 9 hours ago · Like

> ████████ What kinda boat? Good lord! !
> 7 hours ago · Like

Write a comment...   *WhiteWhine*

Gabrielle

IT'S SO WINDY THE BOAT IS VIBRATING AT THE DOCK. WTF WHY IS THIS MY LIFE?!?!?!

about an hour ago · Like · Comment

👍 ████████ likes this.

> **Karolina** ████████ is it lulling you to sleep?
> about an hour ago · Like

> **Rebe**████ http://whitewhine.com/ – A collection of
> first-world problems
> about a minute ago · Like

Write a comment...   *WhiteWhine*

Going Off the *Deep End*

Is there anything better than having a pool? A cool, serene, private sea where clothes are optional, fun is mandatory, and no disgusting ocean creatures can live for more than a few minutes due to the caustic chlorine. Truly, is there anything better than a pool? Apparently, yes: broken bones, car accidents, and most cancers get complained about less than the unbearable, unceasing burden of owning a pool.

The main gripe is about cleaning the pool. It's as if these people believe that once the pool was dug and filled with water, everything would just sort of take care of itself. They must have never seen a pond (or puddle for that matter). If they had, they'd know that water's natural state, when left alone for more than three seconds, is not a crystal clear paradise but a slimy, dark hole that is topped by what looks like the aftermath of an insect genocide. Like the great dinosaurs of yesteryear, looking for relief from the ash and soot, all nature comes to the watering hole to die. Tree frogs, bees, small mammals, turtles, and the occasional frat guy often end their life relaxing to death on the surface of a nice backyard pool. This has caught many a pool owner completely by surprise, though I think pool manufacturers can be forgiven for not including a picture in the catalog.

Some White Whiners, though, don't seem to mind the cleaning the pool so much as they mind the everything else. The fact that the pool sometimes has to be fixed—you know, like any other machine in the world—is an outrage. Or maybe the temperature of the water is either too hot or too cold, turning the owner into a kind of annoying suburban Goldilocks. White Whiners looking to kick up their complaints a notch can even find a way to complain about their pool boys. That notch, of course, is on the Douchebag Scale.

It would be easy to dismiss these beleaguered pool owners as pampered spoiled brats, but I have to caution you. This is one of the only White Whines that should not be met with immediate derision but instead should be met with sympathy. Say, "It must be horrible, all that skimming and changing the chlorine tablets," or "Broken filter? Oh my God, that's just awful!" Why? Because as annoying as pool-related White Whines may be, these people still have pools. I'll gladly listen to someone rage about the expense of the new cover or the look of the crumbling tiles all day, so long as I can do it while I'm drifting on a floating lounge chair, sipping a summery drink, and quietly peeing into the source of all their problems.

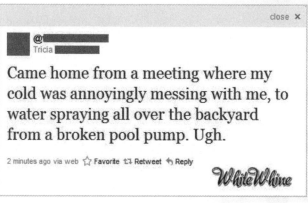

close ✕

@
Tricia

Came home from a meeting where my cold was annoyingly messing with me, to water spraying all over the backyard from a broken pool pump. Ugh.

2 minutes ago via web ☆ Favorite ⇄ Retweet ↩ Reply

White Whine

Really wishes she had a pool in her backyard today (instead of a smelly hot tub).
Like · Comment · Yesterday at 8:50am · ●

White Whine

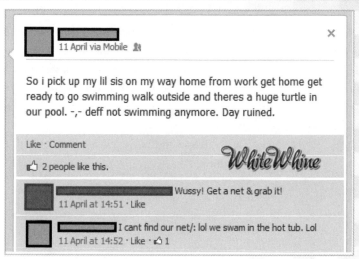

11 April via Mobile 👥

✕

So i pick up my lil sis on my way home from work get home get ready to go swimming walk outside and theres a huge turtle in our pool. -,- deff not swimming anymore. Day ruined.

Like · Comment

👍 2 people like this.

White Whine

Wussy! Get a net & grab it!
11 April at 14:51 · Like

I cant find our net/: lol we swam in the hot tub. Lol
11 April at 14:52 · Like · 👍 1

Horses and Pony *Moans*

There are certain topics that immediately qualify any complaint about them as a White Whine. Caviar, designer sunglasses, tropical islands, and anything having to do with the lack of gluten-free options all qualify. But all of these pale in comparison to the mother of all White Whiney topics: horses.

Horses and humans have had a long, productive history, where horses did all manner of work for our benefit and we rewarded their hard work by eating them in only the most dire of circumstances. This is about as good of a deal as humanity is ever prepared to offer, and it was a great arrangement while it lasted. But ever since we started to build machines to do our dirty work, horses—and let's not forget ponies!—have turned from valuable working animals into gigantic, living, breathing status symbols for the richest of the rich.

Caring for a horse requires an absurd amount of work, so you'd think that there would be a ton of White Whines about the many, many headaches that one must endure while feeding, cleaning, shoeing, housing, breaking, training, and exercising a thousand pound pet. But that's not the case. Horse White Whines are rare gems, much like the rare gems horse owners undoubtedly wear while they take their horse out on its weekly ride. Why is that the case? Well, this author believes that the rarity of horse- and pony-related White Whines has to do with the fact that horse and pony owners almost never are the ones actually taking care of the animals. These owners employ teams of stable hands to do the dirty work.

Lucky for us, though, a few horse and pony owners just couldn't find a stable hand to hold their tongues.

Alexandera ▮▮▮▮
dont you fucking hate when you fall off your horse and bang up your back so you can barely walk and are having trouble breathing?
8 minutes ago · Like · Comment

White Whine

Paula▮▮▮▮▮▮
33 seconds ago 👥

Hate not having a pony to go and play with.. cant wait to get my new one :)

Like · Comment

White Whine

why can't i find a polo club that's close enough and not in jersey? my life is hard
about a minute ago · Like · Comment

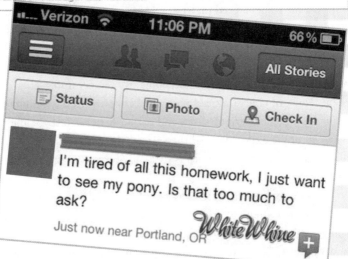

.ıl... Verizon 🛜   **11:06 PM**   66% 🔋

☰   👥   💬   🌐   **All Stories**

📝 **Status**   📷 **Photo**   📍 **Check In**

I'm tired of all this homework, I just want to see my pony. Is that too much to ask?

Just now near Portland, OR   *White Whine* ➕

Kendall▮▮▮▮▮▮
twitvid.com/707XR - WOW just found this video from Christmas 2006! i got my first pony! lol i thiught it was cute, so im showing you
23 hours ago

White Whine

137

White on White:
The First-World on Skiing

Having been surrounded my entire life by enthusiastic skiers—and having been one myself—it's amazing the extent to which a ski trip can become one gigantic White Whine. The gear itself—from the skis to the poles to the 400 other little things you must buy—is extremely expensive, and all of it is made out of some trademarked material meant to keep its users safe and warm on Earth's most punishing summits. Gore-Tex, Thermo-Fleece, and a hundred other "advanced" technologies litter the tags of everything skiers buy, adding to the price and the perception that they will be in complete comfort while ascending to heights—and descending to temperatures—that should kill them. Then, of course, skiers must get themselves to the mountain by car or plane, rent somewhere to sleep, and get a lift ticket just for the privilege of using all of the expensive gear they already bought. All of this initial expense and expectation of comfort leads to some of the more spirited rants you can imagine.

If you only knew about skiing based on Facebook posts or Twitter rants, you wouldn't think it was a leisure activity. Instead, you'd think it was some sort of painful Norse punishment reserved for the wickedest thieves and vagrants. Get caught stealing a pig and the High Viking Council would force you to hand over all of your money and then compel you to ascend and descend an icy mountain for Saturday, Sunday, and half of Dr. Martin Luther King Jr. Day. Tales of icy slopes, sprained limbs, long lift lines, patchy snow, screaming children in ski school, expensive goggles that still fog up, slow gondolas, and a million other inconveniences litter the Internet wherever skiers roam.

Skiers not only become indignant about man-made disasters like the summit bar being too crowded, but also about the state of the mountain itself, as if the owners of Stowe or Okemo ski resorts had been holding back the good, natural snow for a later weekend. "It's all wet and artificial," skiers moan on Twitter, never once stopping to realize how much better that is for skiing than "no snow at all." And God forbid someone goes skiing on an eastern mountain who has previously been skiing out west. To talk to one of these people you'd think that they hadn't actually been skiing in the east, but had been kidnapped and forcibly pushed down a sheet of ice for their captor's amusement. "That's it! Now scratch your new Oakley goggles on those semi-buried twigs, slave!"

But if you ever find yourself listening to a friend bitch and moan about a ski trip and feel the need to punch them in the neck, stop yourself. Remember that for all their obnoxious complaints about the cost, the hassle, the cold, the snow (or lack thereof), the lines, the drive, or the rental house with the all-weather hot tub that didn't even get that hot, there is an underlying truth that will bring a smile to your face: They brought it all on themselves. They paid an arm and a leg—and on a particularly icy mountain, this is often not just an expression—for the privilege of having a horrible weekend.

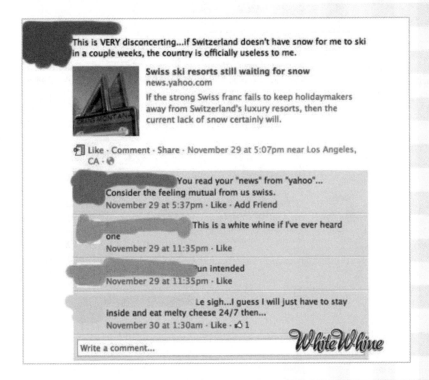

This is VERY disconcerting...if Switzerland doesn't have snow for me to ski in a couple weeks, the country is officially useless to me.

Swiss ski resorts still waiting for snow
news.yahoo.com
If the strong Swiss franc fails to keep holidaymakers away from Switzerland's luxury resorts, then the current lack of snow certainly will.

Like · Comment · Share · November 29 at 5:07pm near Los Angeles, CA ·

You read your "news" from "yahoo"... Consider the feeling mutual from us swiss.
November 29 at 5:37pm · Like · Add Friend

This is a white whine if I've ever heard one
November 29 at 11:35pm · Like

?un intended
November 29 at 11:35pm · Like

Le sigh...I guess I will just have to stay inside and eat melty cheese 24/7 then...
November 30 at 1:30am · Like · 1

Write a comment...

White Whine

Matt
All ski lifts closed, fml

4 minutes ago via Windows Phone · Like · Comment

Matt Lol http://whitewhine.com/
A few seconds ago · Like

Write a comment...

I am so pretentious about when and where I will ski. I am not sorry about it. It is just a fact.

Like · Comment · 2 hours ago near Rochester · 🔒

👍 2 people like this.

I will ski there whenever. I will ski most mountains west of ohio any time. It is these east coast ones that make me cranky and are no fun at all. :\
about an hour ago · Like

My experience is that it is windy, icy, short runs, crowded, expensive, and slow lifts.
about an hour ago · Like

I don't even look at maps on big mountains. I never even learn trail names... I just ski what is in front of me and go where I hear the good snow is.
about an hour ago · Like

really hate having to fly commercial with both ski boots AND golf clubs. #whitewhines
Twitter - 3 hours ago

C
Cant believe I only went snowboarding 26 times this year with a total of 316 lift rides... seemed like I went more!

April 25 at 9:20am · Like · Comment

C a not counting todays lift rides cuz i got the info in the morning when i got there.
April 25 at 9:21am · Like

Write a comment...

Jon
3 hours ago via mobile

I'm skiing in Minnesota right now, even though I've been told not to try it h if I'm used to skiing in the Rockies. Turns out whoever told me that was right.

Like · Comment

👍 5 people like this.

> **Kerri**   Where in MN? Anywhere south of Duluth is pretty crappy skiing hahahahaha
> 3 hours ago via mobile · Like

> **Adam**   I want to be in Minnesota. Lucky
> 2 hours ago · Like

> **Adam**   Well, maybe not now. In like April or May
> 2 hours ago · Like

> White whine
> 38 minutes ago via mobile · Like

Write a comment...

White Whine

I Need a Vacation from
This Vacation

Vacation was something that used to exist before smartphones and e-mail. The idea was that a person could "leave" their work and "relax" somewhere else. Some among us are still able to partake in this decidedly First-World luxury once or twice a year. But sadly these people find that their ability to relax is compromised not by work or pressing matters at home but by the vacation itself. And thus was born one of the most popular and widely used White Whines in history: I need a vacation from this vacation.

There are a number of reasons a vacation can turn from a relaxing jaunt on some foreign shore to an irritating nightmare. Travel delays are common, as nature really doesn't care about vacation plans. Foreign conflict is similarly disruptive, as armed insurgents, like nature, are indifferent to First-Worlder itineraries. Then of course the hotel might be "trashy," the weather might be "shitty," and the Whiner's travel companions might be "fucking annoying." Hopefully a vacationer doesn't get sick because if they do, that resort/city/country will be forever labeled a disease-ridden cesspit.

Even worse, though, is when the destination doesn't live up to expectations. People seem to forget that when traveling, one is in fact "not at home" and, therefore, not always able to live in the precise style to which they've grown accustomed. New restaurants and cuisines are "gross," local traditions are "stupid," and the sights are "boring" or "all the same." The medieval builders who spent lifetimes hoisting stones into place to build Europe's many castles, I'm sure, felt the same way. "Placed the capstone on new castle today. Boring. Looks just like other castle."

The most confounding White Whines that I see from annoyed vacationers is the concern that they are missing an amazing, once-in-a-week-time event at home. Movies premiere, bands play concerts, parties are thrown, all without regard for the poor souls who are languishing abroad, trapped in a verdant, all-inclusive resort. To be comfortably seated in a lounge chair on a tropical island and yet still summon up the discontent to whine about missing a concert back home is baffling. And yet, every day, hundreds of White Whiners do just that.

Maybe these White Whine foreign correspondents have a point. After all, what's the point of a vacation if the vacationer isn't able to relax and enjoy himself? To return home after a trying ordeal abroad, only to go right back into the stresses of work or school seems unfair. I don't like seeing people stressed and annoyed, so I'm going to selflessly offer to go on these stressful vacations in their place.

R██████s
49 minutes ago in Irvine, California · 👥

So, vacation was awesome... but feeling extremely overwhelmed now that I'm back. Thank goodness I get one more vacation in a week and a half! And then coming back will be even MORE stressful! Its a vicious cycle.

1 Like · 6 Comments

White Whine

Comment

I should be gorging on foie but instead I'm waiting on a bus transfer after being rerouted to Bordeaux :(
Like · Comment · 16 minutes ago near Le Haillan, Aquitaine · 👥

██████ · I think you just broke your first-world-problem-o-meter
4 minutes ago · Like

██████ Ha!
2 minutes ago · Like

Write a comment...

White Whine

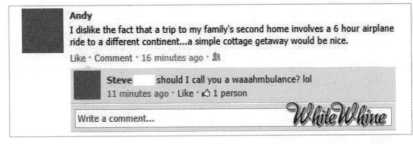

Andy
I dislike the fact that a trip to my family's second home involves a 6 hour airplane ride to a different continent...a simple cottage getaway would be nice.
Like · Comment · 16 minutes ago · 👥

Steve   should I call you a waaahmbulance? lol
11 minutes ago · Like · 👍 1 person

Write a comment...

White Whine

Wish You Were Here . . . Instead of Me

Every year millions of families take to the roads and skies for a little family vacation. For mom and dad, it's a pleasant change of pace from the daily struggle to pay the bills, keep the house in order, and keep up with the monthly sex schedule. For the kids, vacation is a magical event where they'll swim in hotel pools, see incredible sights, and finally experience the wonder of their parents actually getting along. But not every vacation is created equal, and a few White Whiney kids aren't shy about letting their parents know when they've picked the wrong one.

Parents can apparently fail in oh-so-many ways. They can pick a place their kids have already been before and don't wish to revisit, even if that place is an awesome one like the Bahamas or Japan. They can also fail by forcing their poor kids to share a room, which borders on child abuse. I mean, we all got our own hotel rooms on family vacation growing up, right? These horrible parents may even have the gall to cut a trip short and supplement that time with another gift. All horrible outrages, all perpetrated on America's innocent, spoiled little shithead kids. It makes you wonder how their parents aren't locked up in some dingy dungeon, being whipped and burned for the horrors they've visited upon their offspring.

Paradise Lost

People can and will complain about almost any vacation. It doesn't really matter if it's a tour of European cities, a boat trip through Southeast Asia, or a thrilling hike in South America. People will find a way to make these once in a lifetime experiences sound just miserable. But there is no vacation that White Whiners bitch about quite so loudly as those taken at the beach.

I think the reason beach bitching catches everyone's attention is because just hearing the word "beach" brings up wonderful mental imagery. I see palm trees, a gentle breeze, and scantily clad native women serving me fruity liquor drinks while my wife nods in approval. I see complete relaxation and complete contentedness. What I don't see is someone standing in my sun, squeaking about how it rained yesterday, or how the waves are no good, or how it's too hot, or how the resort is full of kids, or how they'd rather be at (insert identical tropical location) than this dump. If I heard these complaints in real life, I'd tell that person to shut up and just enjoy the fact that even though it's not perfect, we're still on the beach, still relaxing, and that my wife is still allowing me liberties with this native girl that I'd never get back home.

Which is kind of what I'd like to say to these White Whiners.

i think i would rather stay home in the cold then go to Jamaica, have to share a room with my parents and my little brother, and on top of that all my sisters are goin to have their boyfriends with them. fml

Like · Comment · a few seconds ago · 👥   *White Whine*

Kevin
I fucking hate Hawaii and all this god damn rain. I'm so fucking tired of it here. Can't wait to get back to America and away from this piece of shit island. Go fuck yourself Hawaii.

📱 2 hours ago via iPhone · Like · Comment   *White Whine*

@_____
Richard_____

No reply from @harpercollinsuk to my complaint about binding quality and paper/size inconsistency in their Samuel Pepys diary series *White Whine*

6 minutes ago via web   ☆ Favorite ↻ Retweet ↩ Reply

The Whitest *Whiners*

Have you heard that saying, "There are baseball players and then there is Babe Ruth"? No? That's because I just made it up to serve as an introduction to this chapter. I hope it catches on. Anyway, just like Babe Ruth was a different, better breed of ball player, so are there superior White Whiners. It's difficult to pinpoint what makes these Whiners so exceptional, but it's like the Supreme Court's definition of obscenity: I know it when I see it.

The tweets and Facebook statuses of these exceptional Whiners just ooze pretension, of which they seem completely unaware. There is no hipster irony in these White Whines. No, these are honest to goodness First-Worlders who are ruminating on the pitfalls of a bad pomegranate, pondering punishments for people who do not know the "rules" of the symphony, and chastising their roommates for thieving their wheatgrass.

If men from the future traveled back in time and wanted to reconstruct the soul of a pampered First-Worlder, this is the source material on which they should base their clones. Which, I'll admit, would be a pretty weird thing to travel back in time to do. But who knows how future people will get their kicks?

$\mathcal{D}own$ on the Ground

Like it or not, there are times when one cannot take a plane, helicopter, or private car from point A to point B. Sometimes one must take public transportation, usually a bus or a train, and take his or her place among the great unwashed. Being that most of us are counted among the great unwashed, this usually isn't a problem. But for someone used to a more sophisticated mode of travel, a bus or a train trip will most certainly be a problem. A First-World Problem, of course.

Though train and bus lines have added amenities like Wi-Fi, White Whiners are quick to point out that the Wi-Fi there is, in fact, shitty garbage that barely works (much like airplane Wi-Fi!). And though they are probably right about the Wi-Fi being shitty garbage, it's not the Wi-Fi that they're angry at. The Wi-Fi, or the dead iPod, or the bumpy ride, is just the easiest thing for more timid White Whiners to focus their anger on. Bolder White Whiners aren't so reserved. They're not afraid to let everyone know that the real problem with the train or the bus is the fact that there are a bunch of other people on it!

Shitty garbage people. Like you. Or me.

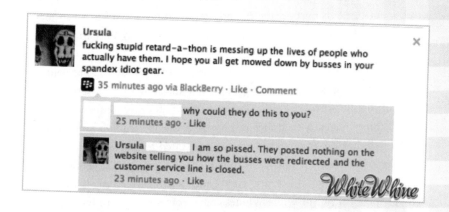

Ugh, *Europe*

Europe, Europe, Europe! The continent that gave us the telescope, democracy, and the works of Shakespeare; also the joust, the automobile, and, of course, white people. Tourists flock to Europe every summer to marvel at this cathedral, and that cathedral, and this other cathedral, and, if we have time, that one cathedral from before. Or perhaps you enjoy buildings that are no longer useful? Europe has you covered! Roman ruins, medieval ruins, and, most recent, economic ruins litter Europe. Literally. If a building drops on the ground, they don't even bother picking it up. Yes, European countries have a unique tempo and culture all their own, something art student expats love and tourists find endlessly irritating. It's why a trip to Europe is always recounted with a caveat, "The Inn was sooo beautiful, but . . . I mean, would it kill them to give you water when you sit down at a restaurant? I shouldn't have to ask for it!" But no complementary water is only the beginning. To the endless irritation of anyone who is not rich enough to afford a two-week jaunt through Europe, the recently returned bring with them so many complaints, large and small, that they probably had to pay for extra baggage at the airport.

The temperature of drinks is often a source of deep disappointment for people visiting Europe: ice must be requested and beer is often served room temperature (the horror!). Public transportation is another frequent source of White Whiner anger, with trains and buses in Europe stupidly not working exactly like they do in whatever city our frustrated tourist is from. Even the generally smaller size of European things—cars, hotel rooms, people, etc.—can elicit a whine, as if the terms "good" and "small" are mutually exclusive. Perhaps the most pitiful White Whines come from students studying abroad, or teens who have been forced to go on family vacation. They pine for the comforts of home, namely TV shows they're currently missing, and the ability to use their phones without incurring massive roaming charges. Outside their hotel room could be the Vatican or the Eiffel Tower, but I think we can all agree that better than seeing either of these would be being able to text their friends as much as they want.

For all the beauty the continent of Europe offers, people can't get past the little inconveniences that Europeans don't even notice. It's like a visit to your parent's house (which, for most postcolonials, it truly is): It's great to see them, but their computer is old and slow, they don't have digital cable, and the fridge is full of weird food. Consequently, Europe is not only the most visited place on Earth, but also the most complained about. But let's not let the Europeans know about this, okay? They already hate us enough.

So today I walked into a Footlocker located in downtown Florence and to my amazement I spotted the White/Varsity Red-Black Jordan 4's. I asked the lady if there was a pair in size 11. The women look's back at me with a smile and says, "Yes we have one last pair!" Without hesitation I tell the lady to bring them out for me to fit and make a purchase. The shoe's felt great, putting the biggest grin on my face. However, after handing back the shoe to lady, she once again, looks back with her hands now in the shoe, saying," why don't you try them on with these new comfortable soles we just got." She rips out the original air jordan sole and shoves the new one in. I stand there in shock... let her know that she fucked up... and depart from the store in a pissed off manner (mind blown). The expression on the ladies face. #priceless. The expression on my face #priceless. Europe doesn't know s**t about jordan's. Jellin like a Felon... not so much *White Whine*

Like · Comment · 8 minutes ago near Florence, Toscana

Dave
August 28 near Florentia, Toscana via mobile

Italy does not run on dunkin and that's not flyin to well with me right bout now

Like · Comment   *White Whine* 6

$\mathscr{U}p$ in the $\mathscr{A}ir$

The ability to fly is undoubtedly one of mankind's greatest achievements, right behind farming, writing, and making cheese. Thousands of years and hundreds of lives went into unlocking the secrets of flight. It has made the world a smaller, more manageable place to live. And though everyone should wonder at the marvel of speeding through the air at hundreds of miles an hour, tens of thousands of feet above the ground, some people just can't get over how goddamn annoying the whole process is. And as much as I might personally agree with some of these complaints, let's never lose sight of the fact that flying is an incredible, luxurious experience. To complain about it is, of course, a White Whine.

The whining starts well before the pilot turns on the seat belt light. It begins with America's last, worst hope against the ongoing threat of terrorism: the TSA. The TSA—or Terrible Stupid Assholes, as I have muttered to myself quietly—are there to protect travelers from any number of airborne threats by "being stupid," "taking forever," and "standing around, doing nothing," according to any number of passengers. Travelers take issue with the TSA's annoying habit of enforcing the rules that, for instance, forbid passengers to bring banned items onto flights. Once past the TSA, the discerning White Whiner will usually have time to lodge one more complaint about how "status" means nothing anymore, and how the Admiral's Club isn't nearly as exclusive as it once was.

Once on the plane, the complaints continue. Though there is an occasional gripe about the food or service, these days most on-board White Whines concern one thing: Wi-Fi. It was only a few short years ago that Wi-Fi on planes became a reality. But that hasn't stopped the wired crowd from immediately attacking its sluggish connection speed. My hunch is that the reason why it's slower than normal Wi-Fi is because when you're using it you're in a metal tube going 700 miles per hour, seven miles in the sky. But what do I know?

No flight, no matter how uncomfortable the seat, how rude the flight attendants, how handsy the TSA agent, can really be that bad. Why? Because the plane took off and landed in a way that caused the passengers not to die. Instead of landing and immediately letting everyone know how terrible the experience was, maybe these White Whiners should consider the fact that they were just flung up into the heavens and somehow came back down again safely, something mankind has spent an eternity trying to accomplish. Even if the Wi-Fi was slow.

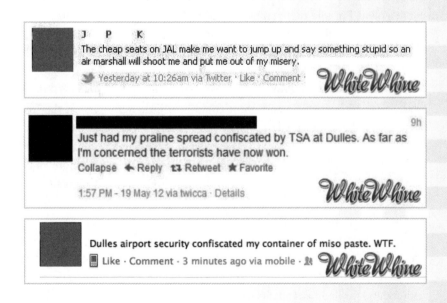

J   P   K
The cheap seats on JAL make me want to jump up and say something stupid so an air marshall will shoot me and put me out of my misery.
Yesterday at 10:26am via Twitter · Like · Comment · *White Whine*

9h
Just had my praline spread confiscated by TSA at Dulles. As far as I'm concerned the terrorists have now won.
Collapse ← Reply ↻ Retweet ★ Favorite
1:57 PM - 19 May 12 via twicca · Details   *White Whine*

Dulles airport security confiscated my container of miso paste. WTF.
Like · Comment · 3 minutes ago via mobile · *White Whine*

First-er *Class*

We've already established that complaining about any aspect of air travel is a White Whine because flying through the air is nothing short of a miracle. But I wanted to make sure I took the time to talk about a subsect of airplane White Whiners who I think deserve extra special treatment. After all, extra special treatment is what they expect. I, of course, refer to those people who complain about flying First Class. Compared to the huddled masses who yearn to breathe (air) free (from the smell of the airplane toilet) back in Coach, flying First Class is an absolute dream. I know, because I've been up there a few times thanks to some well-timed begging at the check-in desk.

The flight attendants are polite, the food is good, the seats are comfortable, and the bathroom is only being peed on—yes, still peed "on" even in First Class—by fellow First Classers. Plus, if everyone seated next to you agrees that it's okay, I'm told that you're allowed to smoke cigars. It's sublime. And yet some travelers find their First Class seats lacking for one reason or another, which is kind of like moaning about a filet mignon not being perfectly cooked when everyone else is eating cold McDonald's.

The main First-World Problem that people up in First Class run into is that First Class isn't quite First enough. It could be a little more First, if they're being honest. In fact, First Class on that other airline is wayyy more First than this First Class. The food could be more First, the blankets could be more First, the service could be more First. The only thing that can't get more First is the place these White Whiners took in the "Most Infuriating Complainers" awards.

That's a real thing, gang.

Now, to be fair, in a few rare instances, a First Class complainer will whine for the exact opposite reason: First Class is too First for them. They're bewildered by the massive amounts of legroom, the endless entertainment options, and the flight attendants who don't treat you like some nagging chore around the house that needs to get done. Maybe these Whiners think this strategy will buy them some sympathy with the rest of us. "Oh look, they're not even having a good flight up in First, poor things." And if only we were all idiots, that might be true.

It's certainly aggravating to hear someone complain about a luxury, but even worse would be to hear that same complaint while you're wedged back in Coach. That's happened to me before. A First Class passenger and his wife had strolled back through Coach to use our bathroom—lucky us!—and I overheard them complaining about how there were only six movies on their complementary personal entertainment centers. Guys, I swear to God, if my voice could have been heard over the roar of the jet engine right outside my window, I would have given them a piece of my mind.

Lewis |
6 minutes ago near Newport, Wales via Mobile

Chew with your mouth shut and chew QUIETLY. I did not buy a first class ticket to listen to your bodily functions. You wouldn't sit there burping or farting would you? Oh and stop drinking red wine, your face looks like a beetroot you old hag.

Like · Comment

likes this.

Saturday

I know this is a total white whine, but the there's so much leg room in business class that I can barely reach the touch screen tv. Life is hard, folks.

Like · Comment · Promote

            and 2 others like this.   *White Whine*

Hotel Haters

Staying at a hotel is the closest most of us will ever come to living like a rich person. Dinner can be brought to your room, kept warm under a cloche (French for "metal dome thing that goes over food"). Plus, you can absolutely trash the place with dirty clothes, dirty towels, and dirty sex, and return to find it spotless. You can even pick up the phone, press "0," demand insane things of the front desk, and then actually have those demands met ("here are your seventeen tiny shampoos, sir"). Plus, hotel experiences almost always happen when one is traveling, which is always an enviable activity for those of us who are not traveling. Yes, hotel living is pretty nice compared to normal living, but not everyone fully appreciates the beauty that is throwing garbage on the floor and knowing someone will be along to pick it up. Some people just don't get it.

Almost all of these hotel haters have run into an all-too-common First-World Problem: The hotel isn't as nice as they expected. Instead of unreserved luxury, they booked luxury on a budget and aren't happy with the results. The pillows are too weird, the windows are dirty, and the chandeliers can't disguise the fact that this place is a straight up dump. Some guests can't even imagine that anyone would enjoy staying at this place, even while they are themselves staying at this place. Amazingly, at least one White Whiner even complained about the maid arranging her beauty supplies in the bathroom. I couldn't figure out why anyone would complain about that until it hit me: her maid back at home must arrange them much better.

I sure do wish they had almond milk at the breakfast buffet at the Hilton... #Hilton #pickyeater

Collapse ← Reply ⇄ Retweet ★ Favorite ••• More

11:44 a.m. - Feb 16, 2013 · Details

WhiteWhine

1 hr

Repl

EH

WhiteWhine

36 minutes ago near Wichita, Kansas · 👥

Dear Avis in Wichita: assigning an Avis chairman a crappy chevy captiva is not an upgrade. I guess it's my fault that my SUV at home has a Cadillac emblem on it and I have exceedingly high standards in the automotive products I drive.

Attn Wichita doubletree: this oversized room that you tried to push off on this diamond as a "suite" is deplorable. Don't tell me the exec suite isn't available when I can see it on my iPad at checkin.

Hospitality workers of Wichita: you're on notice >:-(

Like · Comment

Write a comment...

Post

kanye

Room service uuuuugh! I hate when I order fruit and I can taste the other food they cut with the same knife. Beef flavored pineapples

16 Jan

WhiteWhine

Expensive Car, Expansive Whine

Riddle me this, readers: In tweets that read, "Ugh, I hate my car" or "my stupid car broke down," what percentage of these tweeters are referring to luxury cars? Have you figured it out yet? The answer is zero! That is because if there is something wrong with a luxury car, the owner will never refer to it as "my car," but will instead take pains to always point out what kind of car it is. So, "My stupid car is in the shop again" becomes "My stupid Porsche/Benz/Jag/Tesla/Range Rover/BMW/Audi/etc. is in the shop again."

Luxury car owners can't help name dropping the brand because, to them, this makes the White Whine a little more understandable. They reason that by letting everyone know that (A) their car is in trouble and (B) it cost a ton of money to fix, that should elicit some schadenfreude-like reaction from non-luxury car owners. "Look on Facebook here, Jasper," they imagine us saying. "That poor Jill. Spent all that money on a Porsche and now it's in the shop again! I guess luxury ain't all it's cracked up to be, huh? Anywho, let's get back to coal mining before the boss comes back down into the pit and garnishes our wages for chit chattin'. Also, it's weird how we get Internet down here in the coal mine."

Of course, it's not like that. White Whining about a luxury car produces the exact opposite of sympathy. And if you don't believe me, try reading these complaints and see how you feel afterward.

Nick

I hate Porsche service. Like if my car isn't going to be done when you say then just say you don't know. #idiots

Like · Comment · Share · @█████████ on Twitter · 32 seconds ago via Twitter · 🔒

Damnit. I hate getting into Porsches and forgetting the key slot is on the left side. #facepalm

Like · Comment · 23 minutes ago via mobile · 🔒

👍 4 people like this.

Cap'n

Dear Plainfield and the rest of New Jersey,

When you're finished fixing the lives of those ruined by Sandy, would you mind fixing the roads ruined by stupid potholes and ugly cracks? Please and Thank You!

Sincerely
An Annoyed BMW Driver

Arr! · Weigh in · 6 shots o' rum ago near the fair port o' Plainfield, NJ · 🔒

👍 2 scallywags be enjoyin' this.

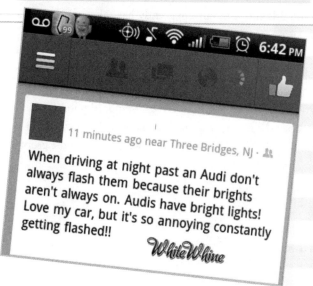

When driving at night past an Audi don't always flash them because their brights aren't always on. Audis have bright lights! Love my car, but it's so annoying constantly getting flashed!!

Beemer *Screamers*

BMW, which stands for something German that probably has some connection to the Nazis, bills itself as one of the finest automakers in the world. Having once rented a BMW by accident (they were out of Hyundais and were forced to give me a huge, free upgrade) I can confirm that they really do drive like a dream. While I was whipping around in my little Hitler-mobile I couldn't even imagine what anyone who owned one of these would complain about. And then I realized that Beemer Screamers almost never complain about the way the car drives (except in the snow). They only complain about when the car needs fixing.

What's particularly funny (for me at least) is that the very things that make BMWs such fantastic cars—the German engineering, the custom parts, the specialty service—ironically make them a huge pain in the ass to fix, according to their owners: They must be taken to a special garage and have special parts installed by special mechanics. All of this adds to cost, which should be obvious with a luxury car, but apparently has taken more than a few BMW owners by surprise.

Now look, I'm not heartless. I completely sympathize with the pain that comes from having to service a car. But to me, complaining about all the extra cost and care that goes into servicing a BMW isn't so forgivable since that's part of BMW lore. It's like buying a standard poodle and then bitching endlessly about the groomer costs. I guess what I'm saying is if you want to drive around in a poodle, you have to be willing to pay the groomer.

Stephen ▊▊▊
Could somebody please bring me a large Hendricks and tonic (with lime) to the BMW of Fairfax waiting room?

January 4 at 2:32pm · 🔒 · Like · Comment

👍 Darla ▊▊▊ and ▊▊▊ like this.

> **John** ▊▊▊ Barbarian. Hendricks and tonic should be garnished with hothouse cucumber slices. I swear, it's like you're living in a tree.
> January 4 at 3:49pm · Like · 👍 2 people

> **Laura** ▊▊▊ oh that is such a good idea
> January 4 at 7:25pm · Like

Write a comment...

WhiteWhine

▊▊▊
Tuesday via mobile 👥

Word of advice. NEVER buy a BMW. If you want service that blows and customer reps who should be locked in a mental institution then be my guest. A little warning for the reps who spoke with me...corporate headquarters got a call, they'll be some layoffs tomorrow.

Like · Comment

WhiteWhine

March 13th

WhiteWhine

If doctor clinics were BMW service shops, every visit for flu shot would lead to recommendation of organ replacement & plastic surgery."

Nat▊▊▊
I hate BMW of roseville they are complete amateurs...my custom part was in weeks ago and never got a call... Now they have to reorder it! This would not happen at sterling BMW! what morons

📧 Like · Comment · about an hour ago via BlackBerry · ⚙

👍 2 people like this.

Write a comment...

WhiteWhine

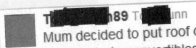

Going *Topless*

The ultimate symbol of luxury is definitely having a private lobster tank in your kitchen. Sadly, not everyone will get to live that beautiful dream and will have to settle for a more cost-efficient luxury. The good news is that ever since the last draft horse was shot and sent to the glue factory we've had the perfect purchase to suit someone looking for affordable ostentation: a convertible. Convertibles are the ultimate middle-class status symbol, since owning one silently implies that their owners are doing so well financially that they ran out of practical things to spend money on. A car they can drive only half of the year, that eats gas, and is extremely unsafe? Sure! "Best $64,000 I ever spent!" they'll chirp as they mash the gas pedal to the floor, while trying desperately to catch their fleeting youth. But after a while something strange happens to the convertible owner. The plastered smile on their face during the first few weeks of topless driving is gone. Replacing it is an exasperated frown and a bevy of White Whines about the trials and tribulations of driving in the elements.

Everything that makes convertibles seem appealing is apparently what makes them a pain in the ass. In my head, driving in a convertible goes like this: I'm cruising down the road on a bright, sunny day, my shades are on, and my hair is being gently blown back while I pump some solid tunes and chat with my beautiful passenger about how grand life is. But according to the veterans of such cars, driving a convertible is nothing like that at all. Hair isn't so much blown, as it is given a jerky, painful hand job, turning a once-stylish coif into a tangled nest of hair. A warm sunny day cannot be enjoyed due to rushing, freezing winds at any speed over three MPH. Sunglasses, hats, and anything not tied down with shark-strength steel fishing wire is

160

likely to be blown onto the highway, never to return. And forget talking or listening to music: No manmade noise, vocal, or electronic can be heard above a convertible's favorite song, "Loud Air Moving Past Your Ears." Convertible owners—and their often vocally annoyed kids—make driving a convertible sound more like an exercise in enduring luxury than a luxurious activity.

But here's the telling bit about convertible complainers: They're still out there driving, every weekend. If driving a convertible was actually as bad as people make it sound, we would have stopped making them in 1915. Nobody would be subjected to a sunburned scalp or direct hit of bird shit right in the face because every car would have a roof. The truth is that driving a convertible is an extremely fun thing to do. But the minor pains that come along with it are too much for owners to ignore, especially considering that they probably spent half a year's salary for the option. But I don't feel bad for them, just like I don't feel bad for the eighteenth-century French aristocrats who "endured" the smell at Versailles Palace in the summer; just like I don't feel bad for the millionaire actress who starves herself for weeks to fit into her Oscar gown; just like I don't feel bad for the traveler who suffered a long, uncomfortable flight en route to the Seychelles. Luxury, no matter how inconvenient, will never elicit sympathy from me.

No matter how tangled their hair gets.

Loaner *Moaners*

Sometimes a car breaks down. That's a fact. And when it does, you have to bring it to a mechanic who will speak gibberish at you and then take away all of your money. That's how it works. But the lucky ones among us—or, really, those who spent more than $60,000 on their car—get to drive a "loaner" car when their car is being worked on. When my car breaks down I leave it in the shop for a few weeks and get to drive a 2013 Nothing, so the idea that my dealership would even give me a free car to ride around in while mine is being fixed seems like a great deal. But like most luxurious things in life, someone will always find a way to complain about it.

That includes being given a free car.

Loaner moaners come off as a particularly needy bunch. I say that because there is an undertone of desperation in their White Whines. They need you to understand that this is not their regular car. They need you to know that their actual car is a far superior ride. More than anything, they need you to understand that they are the victim here.

The victim driving the free car.

While their luxury car is being repaired.

Sara ▮▮▮

BMW, why are you giving me a Jeep for a loner car?

Like · Comment · Share · 48 minutes ago via Mobile · 👥

👍 Melanie ▮▮▮ likes this.

> **Alexis** ▮▮▮▮▮▮▮▮▮ Jeeps are the best!!!!!! 💜
> 38 minutes ago via mobile · Like

> **Sara** ▮▮▮ NOT WHEN IM USED TO A BEAMER.
> 25 minutes ago via mobile · Like

> **Alexis** ▮▮▮▮▮▮▮▮▮ Lol are you kidding? I'd take my jeep over a luxury car any day haha but I like the rough feel. It's definitely no BMW =p
> 24 minutes ago via mobile · Like · 👍 1

> **Sara** ▮▮▮ I'm literally taking it home and switching to the Mustang Lol.
> 24 minutes ago via mobile · Like

> **Alexis** ▮▮▮▮▮▮▮▮▮ Psshh you're crazy haha I LOVE my jeep
> 23 minutes ago via mobile · Like

> **Sara** ▮▮▮ I'm glad you do, and I love my Mustang.
> 15 minutes ago via mobile · Like

> **Alexis** ▮▮▮▮▮▮▮▮▮ Lol I know. Btw, I'm still jealous of your awesome life. Europe... Lol
> 13 minutes ago via mobile · Like · 👍 1

> **Melanie** ▮▮▮ Oh, Sara ▮▮▮ ...you're such a Princess! 😊
> 6 minutes ago via mobile · Like · 👍 1

> **Mandy** ▮▮▮▮▮▮▮▮▮ Seriously? The things they try to pull these days. Whatever happened to customer service.....
> 6 minutes ago via mobile · Like

> **Sara** ▮▮▮ I don't know, Mandy. But I'm suffering for it.
> 4 minutes ago via mobile · Like · 👍 1

Just dropped off the Cayenne to be serviced and they gave me a Boxster convertible as a loaner. The drive sucks. I told my service advisor to reserve a Panamera next time.

1 hour ago near Plano

👍 2 people 💬 6 comments

163

Charitable *Flaws*

One of the nicer things about living here in the First-World is the access to an unending flow of exciting pornography. But another nice thing is that the occasional guilt the well-off feel for being so comfortable spurs them into charitable activities. I can't back this up with numbers because the advance I got for this book wasn't big enough to pay for a researcher, but I'm reasonably confident that America has more charitable institutions than any other country in the world, which, along with our highway system, free market economy, and, again, superb pornography, is something to be proud of. But charity doesn't come easily to everyone, especially not White Whiners.

Some of them find charity very disruptive to their day-to-day activities, even though they're not themselves participating. It's not that they have a problem with the idea or concept of helping others; it's that they wish it could just happen on some other street so they could get to the gym on time. Those people who commit their free time to charity are certainly more admirable, though they're not immune from White Whining themselves. They, too, agree that charity is a good thing, if only it weren't so damn hard.

I don't remember which ancient Greek philosopher held the belief that if the end result is positive, it doesn't matter if the motivation was pure and good (again, not enough money for a researcher), but perhaps that belief rings true here. So long as the poor people got their holiday meal, does it matter if it was dropped off by a despondent White Whiner who wished he was doing anything else besides handing out meals to the poor? Read these White Whines whilst you ponder that philosophical conundrum. And then let's all meet at the Forum to discuss.

My mom is such a jack@$$!!!!!!!

Nov 24, 2011, 9:36:51 AM by ▇▇▇

She made our whole family, go out in the cold, and bring food to poor people. But that's not why I'm pissed. First of all, we had to walk MILES to EVERY SINGLE HOUSE in the FREEZING COLD!!!!!!!!! And my mom thinks that I don't feel good about doing this, and she called me pathetic. I called her an ass, and then she said that wasn't okay. WHAT A F**KING HYPOCRITE!!!!!!!!!! SHE CALLED ME PATHETIC!!!!!!! IS THAT OKAY?!!!!!!!!!! I JUST WANT TO HURT HER SO BAD RIGHT NOW!!!!!!!!!

13 Comments

Mood: 🔴 Rage

The People vs.
the First-World

If I had to pick America's favorite pastime, it wouldn't be baseball or even football; it would be suing each other. Americans love to sue so much that if you watch TV late enough at night, you'll see ads for law firms who specialize in finding reasons to sue. "Do you suffer from joint pain thanks to playing Game Boy in 1991? Do you suffer from anything because of playing Game Boy in 1991? Could you blame any current problem you have on Game Boy in 1991? If you want to sue Nintendo as much as we do, contact the offices of Mitchell, Mitchell, and Korn today." That's a joke, of course. Mitchell, Mitchell, and Korn only deal in celebrity divorces. But the point remains that if you have any problem whatsoever, there's probably somebody to sue over it. And White Whiners have a lot of First-World Problems that they feel someone should pay for.

White Whiners bring some of the craziest lawsuits that the courts have ever had the pleasure of wasting time on. Is Subway withholding an inch from their so-called "footlong"? Better call a lawyer! Can't get that $10,000 ring off your finger? It's definitely not your fatass finger, so you better sue the store that sold it to you! Did the trailer for the movie you were going to see make the movie seem better than it was? Never mind that making the movie seem better than it is is the entire job of a movie trailer. You gotta sue, baby!

A free and just legal system must make space for crazy White Whiners who demand their day in court, but that doesn't make their cases any less funny or any less White Whiney. Just imagine someone living under a brutal military regime that executes dissenters without a trial, learning that over in the States not one, but two people are suing a restaurant over exploding escargot—you'll appreciate living in the free world like never before.

Danville man one of two suing over 'exploding' escargot

By [REDACTED]
Marin Independent Journal
Posted: 11/15/2010 01:36:03 PM PST
Updated: 11/15/2010 01:37:21 PM PST

White Whine

Kids lose "bad mother" lawsuit. Can't take mom to court over bad birthday cards.

by [REDACTED], Shine Staff, on Tue Aug 30, 2011 10:40am PDT

4693 Comments | Post a Comment | Read More from This Author » | Report Abuse

f Share 33K | retweet 261 | Email | Print

White Whine

Woman Sues Chanel After Getting $10,000 Ring Stuck On Her Finger

By [REDACTED] on May 31, 2011 4:30 PM

(Hopelessly Un-Romantic) *White Whine*

Don't you just *hate* it when you slip on a really expensive ring, only to then have to wait several hours in the emergency room for a doctor to pry it off your pudgy digit? I know I do... But I've never gotten so mad that I've sued one of the most famous brands in the world of fashion.

According to the NY Post, a woman from Brooklyn recently popped into the Chanel store in Midtown Manhattan to check out this particular sparkler. And while the bit o' bling went onto her finger sans too much trouble, the same couldn't be said for its removal.

Traffic

Traffic is a measure of how well a society is doing. In a place where almost nobody can afford a car there shouldn't be much traffic, right? So we should all look at traffic jams as the net result of our continued prosperity. But we don't look at it that way because traffic is just the worst. Nobody except the most ardent podcast fan looks forward to a large traffic jam, but, as Americans, we all accept them as part of daily life. Most of us are content to sit for an hour, pass an accident, and be on our way. But for some people, traffic of any nature is simply unacceptable. Why? Because their agenda is more important than anything else in the world.

Yes, it seems nothing is too dire, too important, or too terrible to slow down their commute to work/the gym/vacation. Is the President in town? Well fuck him, that asshole is jamming up the highway! Is there a despondent jumper on the bridge? Hurry the fuck up and jump already! I'm running late here! I can kind of see their point. I mean, a human life is nothing compared to making it to a hair appointment on time, obviously.

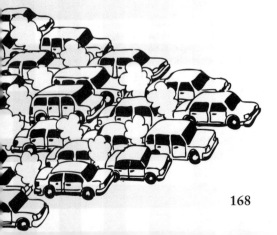

168

Never Forget Whine/11

There is a reason people refer to the pre-9/11 world. Things were different before that day. Everyone was rich and happy, the music was all bland and cheerful, and frosted tips were de rigueur. The events of 9/11 changed everything and everyone, except for Guy Fieri. And now every September 11th we take some time to remember all those who died needlessly in the greatest act of terrorism to ever touch our shores. Surely remembering the fallen—the passengers on the flights, the office workers trapped in the towers, and the courageous cops and firefighters who tried to save them—is something that nobody in their right mind could complain about, right?

Wrong again. For as much as these White Whiners understand the magnitude of the day, they also really don't see the need for all the replayed footage on TV, all the ruined birthdays, and all the traffic jams during the remembrance ceremonies.

Hailey

Dear people on facebook!! 9/11 happened 10 years ago, get over it!! The only ones that should care are the ones that lost their family and friends!! Today is my Mom's and my GodMother's birthday!! And I'm so sick of watching the towers come down every year on this day!! I have read about today in books, but really don't think it should be played every year!!!

Like · Comment · 2 hours ago ·

White History Month

Every February our nation devotes a month to reflecting on the history of African Americans, their many accomplishments and contributions to American society. Nothing will erase the great stains of slavery and segregation, of course, but devoting a month to honoring our great black citizens is generally agreed to be a good first step in moving away from that shameful history. Except that some people out there feel left out. They don't understand why black people get their own month and why white people don't get anything (except everything). You might call these people "racist," but I prefer to call them White Whiners, in a very literal sense.

But they're probably racist, too.

In asking for a month to honor the many accomplishments of white people, these Whiners are overlooking one very crucial fact: Every month in America is white history month because white history is the kind you learn in school. When it comes to creating historical heroes, the white race has been favored by a factor of 100,000,000 to 1. We've even gone so far as to carve four of our favorite white people into a mountain. A MOUNTAIN. People calling for a white history month are basically at an all-you-can-eat buffet and asking to order something off the menu, too.

But maybe I can silence this group of White Whiners once and for all with a simple logic exercise. When you think about it, Black History Month is mainly about white people. If it weren't for white people horribly mistreating black people for the past 500 years, we wouldn't need to have a Black History Month. So in a way, Black History Month is really a month for everyone to remember just how shitty white Americans used to be and learn from our past mistakes and strive to build a more tolerant, equal tomorrow.

And a good way to start would be to stop complaining that there's no white history month.

ali

Can we please have a white history month so we can act as superior as "black" people do in February? #notaracialcomment

← Reply ⟲ Retweet ★ Favorite ••• More

1
FAVORITE

White Whine

9:33 AM - 1 Feb 13

TM

If white people had a history month and black people didnt it would be the end of the fucking world. We should have one too

← Reply ⟲ Retweet ★ Favorite ••• More

6
RETWEETS

White Whine

8:38 AM - 1 Feb 13

Steffanie

February...black history month. Where the fuck is white history month?!? I'd like to celebrate my heritage...

← Reply ⟲ Retweet ★ Favorite ••• More

5
RETWEETS

White Whine

8:41 AM - 1 Feb 13

Hyperbole Is Worse Than the *Holocaust*

Hyperbole is the greatest thing since sex, and nowhere is this literary device used more often than when the middle-to-upper class get frustrated. No annoyance is too small, no complaint too trivial, to be compared to the worst things that have, or can, befall humanity: the Holocaust, rape, the genocide in Darfur, and slavery. When hyperbole of this nature is combined with a White Whine the result is a complaint that is exponentially worse to hear (and to say). Consider this complaint: "I hate Comcast." At best, we could call that a minor White Whine because having cable these days is not really beyond the reach of most wallets. But then add a dash of hyperbole in the mix: "I know what it's like to be a rape victim now. Thanks Comcast!" And there you have yourself a truly offensive White Whine.

Comparisons to the Holocaust are used surprisingly often considering humanity has only achieved that level of institutionalized mass-murder a few dozen times in its entire run. But according to White Whiners across the Internet, the following things are, in fact, worse than the Holocaust: cold showers, folding laundry, and going to school. I don't know about you, but I had no idea that events worse than the mechanized slaughter of six million people were happening in bathrooms, laundry rooms, and classrooms every day.

It really opens your eyes, huh?

As the only republican in this class, I feel like I just survived my own mini Holocaust every time I leave the room.

Like · Comment · about a minute ago via mobile · 👥

Slow internet is my generation's Vietnam. #touringtweets

8 hours ago via Twitter for Mac ☆ Favorite ⇄ Retweet ↩ Reply

Amanda ⬛⬛⬛⬛⬛⬛⬛⬛⬛ 14h

Doing homework in my room is like working in a sweatshop. What the heck.

Expand

That moment when you pour yourself some Cocoa Krispies, and then you realize your milk expired. This is how it must feel to live in a Third World Nation :/

Like · Comment · 6 minutes ago near Los Angeles

👍 Albert ⬛⬛⬛⬛⬛ Melisa ⬛⬛⬛⬛ Veronica ⬛⬛ and 3 others like this.

Alex ⬛⬛⬛ You and your first world problems. >.< Lol.
5 minutes ago · Unlike · 👍 8

Isaac ⬛⬛⬛ ^how the comment has more likes than your status..
4 minutes ago · Unlike · 👍 2

Carlos ⬛⬛⬛ I couldn't stop laughing about that too!

I had to walk to the store like some kind goddamn animal to buy some better milk >.<

http://whitewhine.com/... Lol

White Whine - A Collection of First-World Problems
whitewhine.com
A Collection of First-World Problems, Updated Daily

Japan disaster may make buying Prius difficult. http://on.cnn.com/i3TCAg

about 2 hours ago via web
Retweeted by 100+ people

cnnbrk
CNN Breaking News

White Whine

Foreign Disaster,
Local Tragedy

This being planet Earth, a planet that doesn't seem to like us scurrying around on her face, natural disasters are a part of life. From tornados to earthquakes, hurricanes to tsunamis, nature is constantly trying to rid herself of her finest creation, us. When natural disasters strike, most people bravely leap into action, nobly run for their phones, and selflessly text "HELP" to the Red Cross to make a $5 donation. Sadly, not everyone shows such compassion. A smaller, more . . . how do I say this? . . . shitty group of people react to a natural disaster not with helpful text messages but instead by asking themselves one question: "How will this Malaysian Tsunami/Haitian Earthquake/Japanese Nuclear Plant Meltdown affect me?"

What video game will be delayed because its manufacturing plant is underwater? What car will be delivered late because the factory is ten miles away from a nuclear reactor on the verge of meltdown? What vacation may have to be postponed because the capital city of the tropical island is a smoldering rubble heap? There is a group of people who have the unique ability to turn a decidedly Third-World problem in a far off land into an annoying First-World Problem right here at home. It's almost a skill, to be honest.

If you don't believe me, wait for the next natural disaster to hit (don't worry, one will come). As you're watching it unfold on TV or online, watching the human misery, the destruction of property, and loss of life, try to take

174

one second and think, "But how can I complain about this?" And if you do manage to find some tiny connection to your life—say, like having to pay a bit more for coconut water—try to imagine a scenario in which you voice that complaint in person or online, and then don't go shoot yourself in the face for being the world's worst citizen.

And yet, like clockwork, every time mankind suffers, there is a certain kind of man seemingly suffering much more. Suffering because the new Pokémon game isn't coming in time for Christmas. Suffering because he can't buy a new Prius until next year now. Suffering because yellowtail sashimi is too radioactive to consume. And while I do find natural disasters tragic, I think the real tragedy is that there is probably no afterlife—meaning there probably isn't a hell for these people to burn in. It's not that I want them to suffer the pain of being eternally roasted, so much as I want them to read tweets from people up in heaven saying things like, "Ugh, I wish heat didn't rise! The fires down in hell are making the nectar warm and the ambrosia goopy." Maybe then they'll understand.

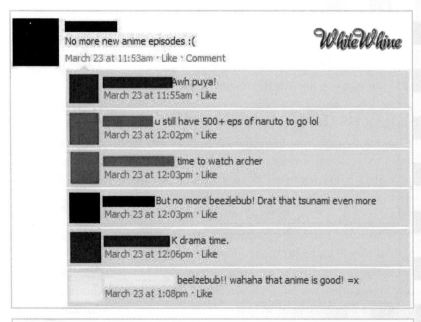

No more new anime episodes :(
March 23 at 11:53am · Like · Comment

> Awh puya!
> March 23 at 11:55am · Like

> u still have 500+ eps of naruto to go lol
> March 23 at 12:02pm · Like

> time to watch archer
> March 23 at 12:03pm · Like

> But no more beezlebub! Drat that tsunami even more
> March 23 at 12:03pm · Like

> K drama time.
> March 23 at 12:06pm · Like

> beelzebub!! wahaha that anime is good! =x
> March 23 at 1:08pm · Like

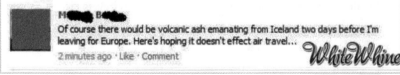

Of course there would be volcanic ash emanating from Iceland two days before I'm leaving for Europe. Here's hoping it doesn't effect air travel...
2 minutes ago · Like · Comment

Hurricane *Pain*

Hurricanes are major weather events in the Atlantic that have the special distinction of getting cute little names. If Mother Nature can sometimes be a bitch, her kids like Sandy, Irene, and Katrina can be even worse. A hurricane whipping through your town can be an extremely destructive event, as I'm sure any insurance company executive will be happy to confirm. Houses are ruined, whole towns are flooded, cars are destroyed, and people are left without electricity for weeks at a time. In short, hurricanes are not to be taken lightly. And these White Whiners aren't taking them lightly, either.

Witness the horror that tinges their tweets as they realize that Starbucks may be closed. Marvel at the raw destructive energy the hurricane must have unleashed to damage the tie-down clip on their hot tub. Weep with these survivors as they tell the heart-wrenching tale of how the hurricane made them miss Pop Punk Fest. Scream to the heavens and ask what kind of God would allow someone to have a ton of Keurig K-Cups but no electricity with which to brew them?!

maids cancelled cause of hurricane irene, thanks media... now I have to clean my house while fasting!

3 hours ago · 👍 1 · Like · Comment

👍   likes this.

    whitewhine.com
4 minutes ago · Like

omfg. really? I have power. and tv. and cable. but cartoon network and bbc america don't work in my room only.

well what's the point of television then?

Like · Comment · 2 hours ago · 🔗

👍 3 people like this.

    I still have no power whatsoever......going on four days today FML
2 hours ago · Like

    this has nothing to do with the power. the channels have been on and off in my room since before. it's just annoying because I've been dying for tv and now I can't watch anything. and I'm obviously not going to call cablevision as they must have enough on their hands as it is.
2 hours ago · Like

    Is there a way you can report it without directly bothering someone (like Atlantic City Electric has an app where you can send in via the app the details of your problem)?
2 hours ago via mobile · Like

    try watching your shows online
2 hours ago via mobile · Like

    I don't think they have that. and   I normally do, but I have literally been bitching about tv for the past few days, it's all I wanted.

suppose I'll just watch more news and depress myself _____.
2 hours ago · Like

🔲 8:48pm

I just realized all my pumpkin spice k-cups will be worthless without electricity ☹

White Whine

177

Shut Up, *Mr. President*

When you're the boss of the biggest company in the world—America—sometimes you have to go on TV and address your 300 million shareholders with important news. The President will pop on the TV to let everyone know that we've killed a terrorist or that he feels for the people affected by the hurricane/flood/tornado or that some psycho just shot up a school in the Midwest. Generally, people want to know what country we're fighting or what tragedy CNN will be talking about for the next month, but the President's irregularly scheduled programming isn't welcomed by 100 percent of the nation. You see, some people just really wanted to watch *The Voice* tonight and don't really care that half of New Jersey is underwater.

What's especially interesting about these Whiners is that the shows they're so upset to be missing are almost always garbage reality TV. Nobody is taking to their social media platforms to complain that Obama just butted into *Breaking Bad* or *Homeland* only to let everyone know that Montana is on fire. Viewers of high-end, character-driven dramas hold their tongues—possibly because they're just going to steal it online when it gets posted to BitTorrent. But the dedicated masses who tune in every week to see which bachelorette gets the rose or which celebrity apprentice gets fired or which two real housewives are going to claw at each other's hair, work themselves into a frothy rage when their shows are interrupted (much like the *Real Housewives*, come to think of it). No tragedy, no momentous political decision, no matter of grave national importance can compete with watching a middle-aged, combed-over clown of a businessman fake-fire a C-list celebrity. The fact is that for some people, real reality is no match for reality TV.

I can't help but wonder if White Whiners like this have always put low-rent entertainment ahead of issues of national importance. When Franklin Roosevelt took to the airwaves to declare December 7th a day that shall live in infamy, was there a flurry of angry telegrams about missing the hysterically racist shtick of *Amos 'n' Andy*? When JFK was letting the nation know that we might be turned into shadows by Russian hydrogen bombs headed to Cuba, did the White House get inundated by angry letters because people missed the antics of *The Beverly Hillbillies*? Come to that, when Abraham Lincoln delivered his beautifully succinct reaffirmation of the cost of freedom at Gettysburg, did a few annoyed locals yell for him to shut up so they could get back to watching . . . cows? I don't know what people did for fun in 1863. I don't think fun was invented until 1923.

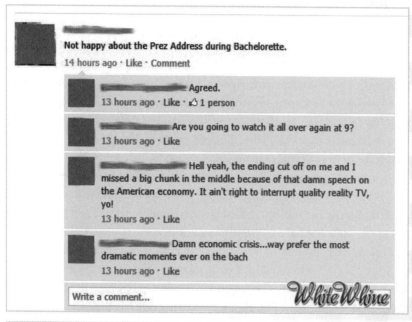

Not happy about the Prez Address during Bachelorette.
14 hours ago · Like · Comment

> Agreed.
> 13 hours ago · Like · 👍 1 person

> Are you going to watch it all over again at 9?
> 13 hours ago · Like

> Hell yeah, the ending cut off on me and I missed a big chunk in the middle because of that damn speech on the American economy. It ain't right to interrupt quality reality TV, yo!
> 13 hours ago · Like

> Damn economic crisis...way prefer the most dramatic moments ever on the bach
> 13 hours ago · Like

Write a comment...

Why are the president/speaker wasting their time on tv? It's not as if viewers can help them. Are they just publicly whining? Make a decision already and stop cutting into our stories.
📱 11 minutes ago via iPhone · Like · Comment

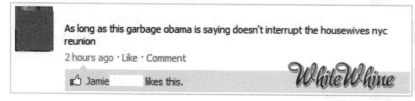

As long as this garbage obama is saying doesn't interrupt the housewives nyc reunion
2 hours ago · Like · Comment

👍 Jamie   likes this.

No Habla Anything Other Than This Language

Almost all human languages are composed of a base language, like Latin, and then regional embellishments to make them distinct. The easiest way to explain this is to imagine languages as being different types of sundaes you could make at a Pinkberry. Related languages have the same base yogurt—like Pinkberry's original "cold sour cream" flavor—but different toppings. If this is how languages are made, then English would be like putting a bit of each yogurt flavor in your cup, then dumping on every single topping, and then, for good measure, adding some of your own toppings you brought from home. This is a very complicated, confusing way to say that English is a complicated, confusing language full of conflicting rules, endless tenses, and words that sound the same but have multiple meanings (like to, two, and too; and fuck, fuck, fuck, fuck, and fuck). You'd think that native English speakers would be a little more understanding that it takes a while for non-native English speakers to master what some linguistics experts have called a "shit-show of words, roots, and rules." But, alas, they (we) are not.

When some people encounter a non-native speaker in any official capacity their immediate reaction is anger. Anger that their phone call with Gap customer service is taking longer than intended, anger that they had to repeat their Chinese food order twice, and, secretly, anger that they can't be one of those people who can switch to flawless Spanish or Mandarin or French when needed, like a sexy, jet-setting spy. Behind every White Whine about the long, frustrating process of negotiating with the landscapers in Spanglish or trying to give the Polish maid specific instructions on how to wash little Tyler's soccer uniform is an underlying sense of inferiority. Because the truth is, behind the frustrated face of every ESL speaker is someone who has a S L, while most of the loudest complainers simply have E.

Just as the former high school football star (and current overweight alcoholic townie) will be the loudest critic at the high school football game, so too will people with only the English language under their belt be the first to criticize those people they're attempting to communicate with. It's insecurity, plain and simple. And I know this because I am one of those people. I took three languages in school, and the highest grade I ever got in any of them was "See me after class." If you have even the slightest accent in your English you might as well be speaking your native tongue, because that is how it will sound to me. I'll attempt to keep the conversation alive with a few catchall responses like, "Yeah, you're telling me!" and "Huh, that's interesting," but we both know the score. We both know we won't be debating politics anytime soon, because I'll think you were asking me who I "bloated whore in the last erection."

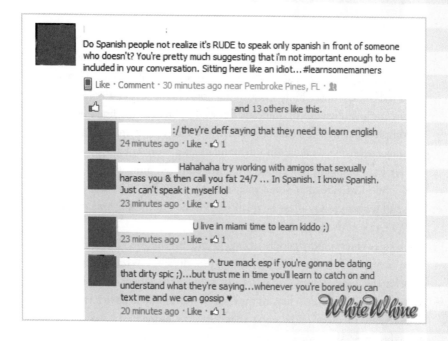

Feminisn't

Sometimes I wonder if husbands in the 1950s ever realized just how good they had it. All they really had to do was go to work and make money. They weren't expected to help raise children, clean the house, shop, cook, do the laundry, or do any of the thousands of domestic duties that I frequently find myself failing to complete to my wife's exacting standards. Those days are long gone thanks to brave, assertive women who demanded, and won, equal opportunities in our society, changing our country for the better in almost every single way. And while I'm sure that some men secretly long for the Honey-I'm-Home days, all women today must be thrilled with their accomplishments, right?

Well, not all women, no.

Just as some wealthy people strangely pine for the good ol' days when they were poor and worried all the time, so, too, do some White Whiney women pine for the days of domestic servitude. Why, they wonder, are they expected to work and contribute when all they really want to do is have a rich husband to take care of them? Why can't they just stay home and cook a bit? Why does this oppressive society of ours demand that they get an education and make something of themselves?! If you can think of a better White Whine than complaining about all the opportunities afforded to you in this world, have at it.

sometimes i wish women didnt have rights, so then i could just be baking cookies instead of studying for finals.
Thu Dec 09 2010 15:58:22 (CST) via web

WhiteWhine

 Gisell G

Why did females have to fight for equal rights? I think it would've been easier to be a house wife and let my man work for the money.

📱 2 hours ago via Mobile Web · Like · Comment

WhiteWhine

 May 2 via mobile 👥

Can I just find a husband so I can go ahead and quit college please?

Like · Comment

👍 and 26 others like this.

💬 View all 17 comments

WhiteWhine

Handicapped People:
Disabling the Rest of Us

When we were cave folk and someone broke their leg, we probably just left that dude on a rock as bait to lure in saber-toothed tigers. We've come a long way since those days. For starters, we killed all the saber-toothed tigers (smart move, us), and we've created a society where immobile people can still lead fulfilling, meaningful lives. Most normal, not-horrible people willingly "suffer" the small inconveniences that a handicapped accessible world imposes. We wait the extra minute while a handicapped person gets on the bus or park our car on the other side of the lot so that a person in a wheelchair can get to a store more easily. But there are some people out there who wish we were still doing the saber-toothed tiger bait thing.

And make no mistake about it, these people are White Whiners. A particularly disgraceful group of White Whiners, to be sure, but White Whiners nonetheless. You just have to put yourself in the handicapped person's shoes to see why. If you were handicapped, being fully mobile would be the ultimate luxury. You'd gladly park on the other side of the lot or happily wait the extra minute while the handicapped person got on the bus. So for able-bodied people to complain about the inconvenience of living in a world with non-walking people is really the ultimate White Whine.

And if this doesn't really make sense, I hope you'll forgive me. I kind of was just looking for an excuse to call these people out.

Kyle And I only support helping the needy to a point.. If you play the lottery that is getting pregnant, you know the risks, and if you have a retarded kid, I shouldn't have to pay for it its entire life.. I don't make decisions that you have to pay for. The way it is now, if you have a retarded kid, that kid goes on Social Security from day one.....and they haven't paid a dime into it....

4 hours ago · Like

WhiteWhine

Mike

You're right im not handicap....but im obviously not moving my car...so shut up you fat ugly bitch

Like · Comment · 2 hours ago near Whitesboro, NY ·

👍 5 people like this.

 quit bein so nice Mike
about an hour ago · Like

Mike ⬛ Haha!
about an hour ago via mobile · Like

WhiteWhine

Sammy ⬛ wow seriously? i've been inline for space mountin for at least forty five minutes but a guy in a wheelchair gets to go straight to the front. next spring break im going to six flags.

12 hours ago · Comment · Like

WhiteWhine

Why does this guy get a "handicap plate" because he's missing a hand???.....not tryin to be rude or anything, and I sorta feel bad for him but isnt this abusing the "plate" advantage???...this guy can walk faster to the TARGET door than I can....and whats worse is he knows hes up to no good...can see it on his face.....just all "yup i got the "plate" and theres nothing you normies can do while i skip to the front door"....i dunno, i guess when life gives you a "free-be" you take it and run...well played i suppose

Like · Comment · 7 minutes ago · ❄

WhiteWhine

The Horror of the
Homeless

When it comes to the homeless, White Whiners react one of two ways: with anger and disgust, or with envy. The first group views the homeless the way you or I might view a bee that is stuck inside the car: a moderately dangerous, irrational creature we wish wasn't here right now. Among the homeless-hating sect, every action—including the action of just being homeless—is a threat to either their body or society at large. Asking for change is annoying, sleeping in garbage is terrifying, and seeing a homeless person commit the major crime of digging through the trash for something to eat is repulsive and criminal. The compassion that most humans are programmed with apparently doesn't extend past a certain income level for these White Whiners. What makes them White Whiners (and not, say, normal assholes) is that the way they treat the homeless speaks to their larger view of the world: They believe it is unfair that they should have to share a world with the likes of the homeless. If this is not a White Whine, then what is?

And then there are the envious White Whiners. This group, though not as outright cruel as the previous, is more into belittling the plight of the homeless. They "envy" the homeless's carefree, easy-going lifestyle; and they pine for the chance to trade in their stressful lives for ones where they don't know where they're going to sleep or what they're going to eat that night. Oh, if we could all be as free as the guy passed out in the alley! To believe for even a second that a life with (A) a home, (B) money, and (C) not fighting rats for food is in any way worse than being homeless is, of course, a White Whine.

And if these White Whine complaints make you feel terrible about humanity, don't fear. Homelessness has been around since the birth of civilization. Jesus Christ was born in the ancient equivalent of an auto repair shop, after all. So even if we can't teach everyone in the world to look at the homeless as people and not humanoid animals, at least we'll have the satisfaction of knowing that there will always be homeless people around to annoy those White Whiners.

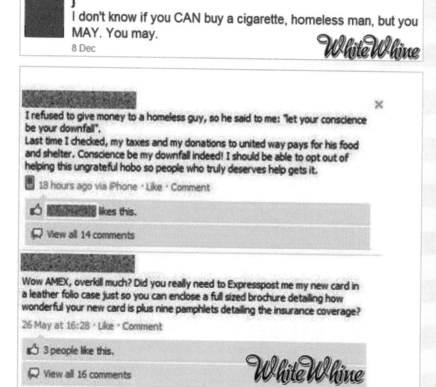

j
I don't know if you CAN buy a cigarette, homeless man, but you MAY. You may.
8 Dec

I refused to give money to a homeless guy, so he said to me: "let your conscience be your downfall".
Last time I checked, my taxes and my donations to united way pays for his food and shelter. Conscience be my downfall indeed! I should be able to opt out of helping this ungrateful hobo so people who truly deserves help gets it.
18 hours ago via iPhone · Like · Comment

👍 ████ likes this.

💬 View all 14 comments

Wow AMEX, overkill much? Did you really need to Expresspost me my new card in a leather folio case just so you can enclose a full sized brochure detailing how wonderful your new card is plus nine pamphlets detailing the insurance coverage?
26 May at 16:28 · Like · Comment

👍 3 people like this.

💬 View all 16 comments

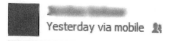

Yesterday via mobile

Nothing pisses me off more than a street bum paying for his shitty steel reserve beer in change and holding up the line in the gas station. I hope this bastard gets shanked under his bridge tonight.

Hipster *Bashing*

I remember when I first heard the term "hipster." It was in the early 2000s, and my college roommate described a kid he was making fun of as being a hipster. I asked what a hipster was, and he said a skinny white kid who wears tight clothes and deliberately moves to a rough neighborhood. That sounded strange to me at the time, and then I blinked and realized that half of New York City's residents fit that description. Having lived among the hipsters for a decade now, I can tell you that they're really not that bad at all. They open good restaurants where they pickle their own everything; they listen to great music, though by the time you discover it, it isn't great anymore; and they are generally interesting people, even if almost none of them will own up to the label "hipster."

But there was one hipster who decided to own it. One lone hipster voice cried out on behalf of all the other hipsters out there who were afraid to come out of the closet (that they built themselves out of wood they found while dumpster diving in Brooklyn). One brave hipster who not only declared himself a hipster but also spun a yarn (figuratively, and probably literally as well) about being a member of this most oppressed group of citizens. He may never live to see his hipster brethren accepted as important parts of the social fabric, but that doesn't matter. What matters is that someone has finally spoken up on behalf of the voiceless, downtrodden hipster and declared that he will not stand for discrimination anymore!

Maybe this guy is the reason no hipster wants to call him or herself that?

Them: "What a hipster."

Me: "If by hipster you mean to say that I take pictures of my food, sunsets, various things/occurrences/occasions in my life, etc. on Instagram, wear cardigans, scarfs, skinny jeans, and Toms, then yes. I am what you say."

I'm getting really tired of the term "hipster" becoming a derogatory name to call everybody and everything. "Hipsters" are no less of a person than you are.

"We" wear clothes as you wear clothes. Eat as you eat. See as you see. We all just do our thing a little differently. Personally, I like the style of clothing that "hipsters" wear. And Instagram interests me. Big deal. Why is that such a bad thing?

Just because you may not feel the same way I do does not give you permission to talk to me or of me like I am inferior.

So know that as hard as it may be sometimes to listen to people talk dishonorably of me, I can say that I have never lost respect for anybody. I may not get treated rightly, but that doesn't mean I shouldn't treat you rightly. But really. You should get on with your life and stop talking about me anyway. There are much greater things to discuss then of people.

Like · Comment · about an hour ago near Little Boston · 👥

👍 19 people like this.

: Preaccch
about an hour ago via mobile · Like · 👍 2

WhiteWhine

Is your last paragraph really necessary? Don't act like hipster's the new n word or anything really that derogatory.
about an hour ago · Unlike · 👍 2

Gamer *Grief*

From simple, humble beginnings, video games have grown to become the dominant form of entertainment for children ages ten to thirty-five who like to call each other "fags" on Xbox Live. When I first encountered video games in 1989 there was nobody to call a fag except the dog in Duck Hunt, and he just laughed no matter what. I bring this up to highlight how far the art of video games has progressed in the last thirty years. And yet for all of that progress, game designers still can't seem to make a game or system that gamers won't whine about.

The more complicated and intense the systems get, the more complicated and intense the White Whines have become. In the olden days if a system wasn't working, you simply took out the cartridge, blew on it really hard, and put it back in. If that didn't work, you hit it a few times with your hand or a rolled-up copy of *Nintendo Power* magazine. And if that didn't work, you assumed your little brother broke it and had your friend hold him down while you farted in his face until he admitted to touching your stuff. It was a simpler time.

These days, systems require updates and complicated software patches in order to continue to waste your time as efficiently as possible. These updates, plus system downtime and any bugs that happen to appear in games or software, are responsible for the majority of video game White Whines. And, boy, people do not have a lot of patience when it comes to not playing video games.

I like to imagine these Whiners while anything else in their life is getting patched, updated, or repaired. For instance, I like to imagine one of them standing behind a mechanic who's putting new brakes on his car, screaming about how "it's so fucking stupid" that a car "needs new shit, like, all the time!" Or on a surgeon's table while he has a new knee being put in, moaning about how he just wants to go back to walking around already, Jesus! Or even at the birth of his first child: While his wife screams in agony trying to update their family with a new title, he sends out a barrage of tweets about how he's excited to play with the new title, but how come it's taking so long for it come out.

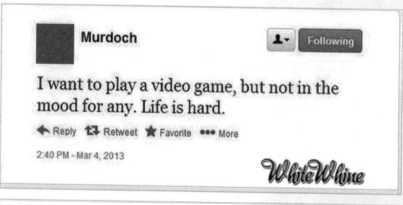

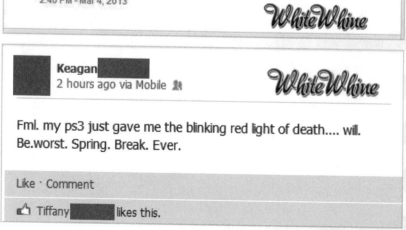

13 minutes ago via mobile

Only good thing about the Xbox failure thanks to  is I can catch up on the tv shows i haven't been watching

Like · Comment

 6 hours ago via mobile

Well my car shut off my Xbox during an update and now needs to be repaired .. No Xbox for at least 2-5 weeks great now ill really have nothing to at home

Like · Comment

 Shouldn't have sold your old one
5 hours ago via mobile · Like

 U can cook n clean lol
20 minutes ago via mobile · Like

 Write a comment...

 8 hours ago via mobile

You have to update your dashboard to play online that's so retarded and as usual mine won't fucking update I love bullshit in the morning

Morgan

god this stupid new pokemon game means i'll have to get a stupid new handheld video game system in 10 months ugh

Like · Comment · 6 minutes ago near Minneapolis, MN ·

 Write a comment...

White Whine

 Justin ████████
May 27 🌐

Just found out that my video card does not support Diablo 3. FML.

Like · Comment · Share

👍 3 people like this.

 Ron ████ im in the same boat
May 27 at 11:38pm · Like

 Ciara ████ First world problems.
May 27 at 11:39pm · Like · 👍 2

 Benjamin████████ its an awesome but different game
May 27 at 11:40pm · Like

████ **Hammers**◢ Quit sucking dick. You will be fine
May 27 at 11:43pm via mobile · Like · 👍 2

White Whine

---

1 note   reblog   💜

My parents are buying me a car for my birthday and im gutted because i wanted batman arkham city instead :(</3

#ps3

White Whine

193

It's My Birthday, and I'll Whine if I Want To

Birthdays may be one of the only things in the world that simultaneously makes you special —since, hey, it's your birthday!—and makes you completely ordinary—since, hey, everyone in the world has a birthday. Birthdays are traditionally celebrated by getting extremely drunk and then texting your ex. They're also celebrated by people giving cards and gifts, though recently the ease and convenience of simply posting "Happy BDay!" to the birthday boy or girl's Facebook wall has become the de facto way to wish someone well on their special day. And yet even here we find White Whiners who, like angry gods, are unsatisfied with a simple tribute.

Some White Whiners get upset because their friends failed to wish them a happy birthday via their Facebook wall. Some White Whiners are upset because too many of their friends wished them a happy birthday on their Facebook wall, making it all feel so impersonal. And still more White Whiners are just upset because . . . who knows? I guess because you can act like a total ass on your birthday and get completely away with it. For example . . .

Salina ▮▮▮▮▮
22 hours ago near New York 👥

is so grateful to have wonderful friends who took the time to wish me a happy birthday...it truly helped to make my day special – thanks! To the "friends" who were on and couldn't take the time to write a quick post..well...let's examine the word in the quotes...

Like · Comment

👍 ▮▮▮▮ likes this.

> **Tracy** ▮▮▮▮ and some of us have all the alerts turned off. hope it was good.
> 21 hours ago · Like

> **Allison** ▮▮▮▮ Happy Belated!
> 21 hours ago · Like

> **Salina** ▮▮▮▮ Thanks guys!!
> 21 hours ago · Like

> **Mary** ▮▮▮▮▮▮▮ some have been in complete disarray with the power being out and lives turned upside down....hope you had a great birthday 😊
> 18 hours ago · Like

Please only wish me "happy birthday" if you can do so creatively! I don't want 300 comments on my wall that say "happy birthday". Thanks to everyone so far for the b-day wishes.
21 minutes ago · Like · Comment

I just facebook thanked the 113 people who wished me happy birthday on my facebook wall. This is why I usually deactivate my facebook the day of my b-day. lol.
about an hour ago · Like · Comment

Fuck You,
Mom and/or Dad

It must be hard being a parent today. Gone are the days of "be a man," "get out there and win," and "get me a beer, boy." Modern parents must be nurturing, loving, supportive, endlessly patient, never angry, and completely devoted to the sole task of giving their child every single thing he or she desires. When they fail in that regard—or when they succeed, but not to their child's exacting standards—their kids are not going to hold back the White Whines.

A parent cannot win. If a parent chooses to withhold a luxury, perhaps in an attempt to teach a lesson about value or hard work, they are accused of being cheap or unloving. If they give in and buy their White Whiney kids that luxury, they'll just be doing what is expected and nothing more. If the parent attempts to discipline their child by taking away a treasured possession—like an iPhone or a Tumblr account—they're accused of basically being Hitler. Worse than Hitler, really. Imagine Hitler, but in addition to the genocide and war, he's going around taking away kids' iPods.

Even the most legitimate complaint from a kid growing up in the First-World is annoying for the sole fact that a few decades ago, just making it through childhood was an accomplishment. Adults have spent billions of dollars and thousands of years trying to figure out how to keep the maximum number of kids alive and well, and for what? To get called a dumb old dickhead by their kids when they use the wrong laundry detergent?

5 boats, yet my parents still wont let me take them out. #Trustissues

Share

👍 ████████████████████████ this.

WhiteWhine

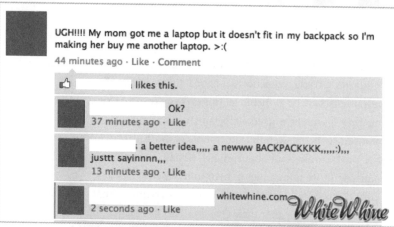

UGH!!!! My mom got me a laptop but it doesn't fit in my backpack so I'm making her buy me another laptop. >:(

44 minutes ago · Like · Comment

👍 ████████ i likes this.

████████ Ok?
37 minutes ago · Like

████████ a better idea,,,,, a newww BACKPACKKKK,,,,,:),,, justtt sayinnnn,,,
13 minutes ago · Like

████████ whitewhine.com
2 seconds ago · Like

WhiteWhine

Gave Daddy an ultimatum: buy me a car or a longboard for college. He's leaning towards a car.. Do I rly look THAT uncoordinated?!!! #sigh

5 minutes ago via Echofon

Reply   Retweet   More

WhiteWhine

Just Die *Already!*

Grandparents are like parents except older, wiser, and fartier. Everyone has them—or, more often than not, had them—and each one accounts for one quarter of your genetic makeup. I don't think it's any big secret that grandparents can be difficult at times. They're often sick, we worry about them, they frequently need help, and a good number of them are deeply committed to being Republican, racist, or both. But we love them because that is what family is all about, right? Wrong. For some people, grandparents are nothing more than a big ol' pain in the ass.

Grandkids usually take issue with one of two things: that their grandparents are alive and gross or that their grandparents are dead and cheap. Those who dislike their living grandparents can't seem to wait for death's icy fingers to whisk them away so they don't have to deal with the general unpleasantness of having someone old and infirm in their life. But once death comes and carries grandparents off to that giant The Price Is Right game in the sky, some grandkids find that what was left behind just isn't enough. After all, these grandparents had decades and decades to build up a fortune to leave behind, so what the hell happened to it all?

When I see these White Whines I want justice. I want these grandparents to write their shitty little grandkids out of the will. I want their grandkids to feel the sting of an elder scorned from beyond the grave. I want the old and infirm to have the last laugh, and for the young and whiny to taste the sour punch of an angry old relation. But I know that won't happen. I know these grandparents will go to their grave never having the slightest idea of what their grandkids think about them. Why? Because for all of their wisdom, they just can't seem to figure out "that damn compu-box thing in the den."

2 💬 📷 ♥

my uncle died and now i have to wear all black for a while! wtf its summer! i can't wear black in cancun

White Whine

---

34 minutes ago near ▮▮▮▮▮▮▮

My grandad left my mum his Audi in his will. What about my need for an Audi grandad?! WHAT ABOUT MY NEEDS.

Like · Comment

> I'm sorry for your loss.
> 4 minutes ago · Like

> ...
> 4 minutes ago · Like

Write a comment...

White Whine

#Thatawkwardmomentwhen my grandmother is gross and sick in the bathroom for ten minutes and then wants me to go in. #Lolno

14 hours ago

White Whine

White Whine ...   ← Reply ⟲ Retweet ★ Favorited · Open

I feel the bad economy. I received my xmas check from my grandmother... this year she gave $100.. last year it was $1,000.

Raising the Next Generation of *Whiners*

White Whiners are not born, they are bred. The process of becoming a White Whiner begins very young, while the child is still in diapers, in fact. At this impressionable age, children are taught the value of brand-name diapers, organic baby food, and a thousand other little luxuries that will almost always fall short in one way or another. Although the child will not understand the concept of "value" or "premium" as she takes a wet dump into a biodegradable $11 diaper, perhaps she will pick up on the subtle look of smug satisfaction on her parents' faces when they pull out a fresh diaper and make a point of showing it around to the other parents before strapping it on. The kind of look that says, "If only you loved your child as much as I do mine, maybe then you'd be willing to spend the money on the best diapers."

As we've learned through a century or two of developmental psychology study, a child learns to mimic his or her parent. White Whiner parents who bitch about the quality of the day care center or the sweetness of the apple juice served at preschool are doing their part to ensure that their child will grow up to feel the same way. It also ensures that those same proud parents—the ones who insisted on the best in everything for their kids—will soon be the victims of their own creation. Like Dr. Frankenstein or the Grizzly Man, the little White Whiner they loved and trained will soon turn on them. The child has been taught to expect the best in everything, but rarely do his or her parents realize that this desire includes the best in parental figures as well. As it was impossible for any organic diaper company to live up to the expectations of the parent, so will it be impossible for the parent to live up to their White Whiner's expectation of them.

Because of these parents, the world will always be well stocked with White Whiners. For someday, many years from now, that child will make a child of his or her own, buy that child the best in everything, teach that child to expect perfection, and, hallelujah, the cycle will begin again!

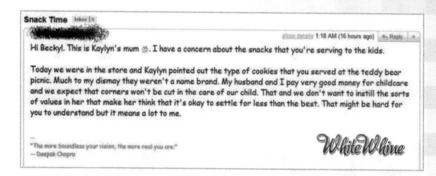

Snack Time Inbox | X

show details 1:18 AM (16 hours ago) | Reply |

Hi Beckyl. This is Kaylyn's mum 😊. I have a concern about the snacks that you're serving to the kids.

Today we were in the store and Kaylyn pointed out the type of cookies that you served at the teddy bear picnic. Much to my dismay they weren't a name brand. My husband and I pay very good money for childcare and we expect that corners won't be cut in the care of our child. That and we don't want to instill the sorts of values in her that make her think that it's okay to settle for less than the best. That might be hard for you to understand but it means a lot to me.

--
"The more boundless your vision, the more real you are."
— Deepak Chopra

White Whine

Donna

Planning family summer vacations are getting harder these days. The girls turned down Belize and Puerto Rico. All they wanted was to go to San Diego. lol I love S.D., but I wasn't so willing to give up my tropical summer vacay! ;-) Negotiations went well, we agreed on Kauai. bahaha Can't wait for June!

Like · Comment · 18 minutes ago ·

White Whine

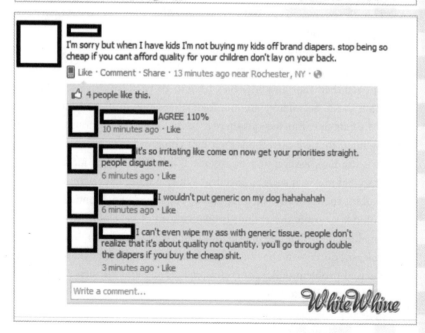

I'm sorry but when I have kids I'm not buying my kids off brand diapers. stop being so cheap if you cant afford quality for your children don't lay on your back.

Like · Comment · Share · 13 minutes ago near Rochester, NY ·

4 people like this.

AGREE 110%
10 minutes ago · Like

it's so irritating like come on now get your priorities straight. people disgust me.
6 minutes ago · Like

I wouldn't put generic on my dog hahahah
6 minutes ago · Like

I can't even wipe my ass with generic tissue. people don't realize that it's about quality not quantity. you'll go through double the diapers if you buy the cheap shit.
3 minutes ago · Like

Write a comment...

White Whine

I Don't Want to *Dye*

There are certain things that often provoke an overreaction. Your favorite team winning the big game may cause you to burn a car, for instance. Or someone holding up their index finger while they finish texting to let you know they'll be right with you may cause you to bite their finger off. These are extreme examples, of course, but our next group of White Whiners fall squarely in the overreacting camp. They are people who have dyed their hair and, boy, do they want you to know about it.

Hair dye crying can be done for any number of reasons: They don't like the dye job they just got; they miss their old color; the dyist (?) was rude; they just dyed their hair and now they have to go back to their old color for a modeling shoot. See! There are hundreds of reasons someone could whine about their hair dye. But they all share a common misconception that is lost on the Whiner: that we care about their hair color.

That is the base assumption of anyone White Whining about a dye job, and that's what makes it such an excellent White Whine. They want the world to feel bad for them because their hair came out strawberry blonde instead of regular blonde or came out walnut brown instead of hazelnut brown or just came out altogether (that one may actually be a legit complaint). But we don't care—at least I don't—and having a slightly different color hair than intended isn't an actual problem which, of course, makes any and all such complaints a bleached blonde White Whine.

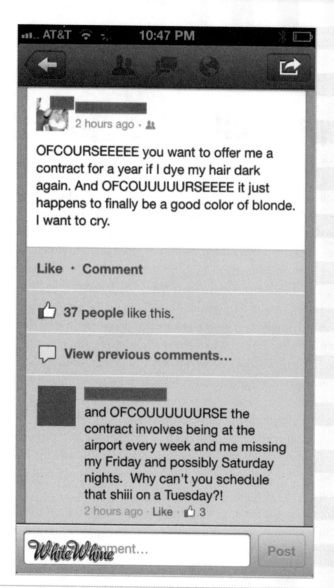

2 hours ago · 👥

OFCOURSEEEEE you want to offer me a contract for a year if I dye my hair dark again. And OFCOUUUURSEEEE it just happens to finally be a good color of blonde. I want to cry.

Like · Comment

👍 37 people like this.

💬 View previous comments...

and OFCOUUUUUURSE the contract involves being at the airport every week and me missing my Friday and possibly Saturday nights. Why can't you schedule that shiii on a Tuesday?!

2 hours ago · Like · 👍 3

WhiteWhine ment...   Post

2h

i think one of the hardest things ive done in my life is from being bright blonde to going dark brown #ripblonde   *WhiteWhine*

Expand

$\mathcal{N}ail$ Fail

We used to have cool claws on our hands and feet. Then we evolved into helpless weaklings and our formerly awesome claws became lame little toe- and fingernails. When you have claws all you need to do is occasionally nibble at them to create a nice, sharp point. But when you have nails, they require constant care to keep them healthy, strong, and, most important, French tipped. This process, called either a manicure (hands), a pedicure (feet), or a mani-pedi (combination, as said by someone who watches too much *Real Housewives*), should be a relaxing exercise in pampering. Often though, it goes horribly, horribly wrong. Or whatever the equivalent to "horribly wrong" is when talking about someone who paints your finger- or toenails.

Manicurists can be too rough on our Whiners' dainty hands and feet, causing discomfort (which has been par for the course since I began cutting my finger- and toenails). Manicurists may even have the gall not to be perfect at painting nails, an embarrassment that a whopping zero people will notice. If our customer is truly unlucky, she may even get stuck with the worst kind of manicurist of all: a white person. If you get a white person, that is apparently bad news. Why? Nobody knows.

Complaining about any pampering is of course a White Whine, but there's something about a mani-pedi whine that's a little more absurd. I think it's because the Whiner is seated upon a throne-like high chair while someone crouches below, washing, rubbing, and generally pleasuring the Whiner's feet. I can imagine a king or queen in that same position, uttering the same complaints. "Peasant! Your touch is too rough about my gout-swollen feet!" the queen would shout, while striking the peasant with a cane. These days, we don't strike manicurists with canes, but rather with a low rating on Yelp. Which is much more effective.

Susan ██████
I hate when I go for a manicure and get stuck with the only white employee. Just my luck.
Like · Comment · Unfollow post · 23 minutes ago

👎 _____ and 2 others like this.

WhiteWhine

July 2 via mobile 👥

It's really inconvenient when I like one nail salon for my fingers and another for my toes....

Like · Comment   👍 4 💬 3

👍

As Scott would say - #firstworldproblems
July 2 at 4:10pm via mobile · Like · 👍 4

totesss
July 2 at 4:29pm via mobile · Like

life is rough
July 2 at 6:58pm · Like

Write a comment...   *WhiteWhine*

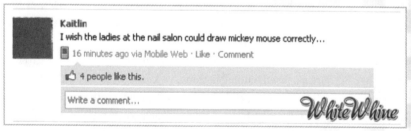

Kaitlin
I wish the ladies at the nail salon could draw mickey mouse correctly...
📱 16 minutes ago via Mobile Web · Like · Comment

👍 4 people like this.

Write a comment...   *WhiteWhine*

The Problems with
Pampering

Pampering is something that humans have been into since it consisted of picking and eating mites off each other's backs. These days, we don't eat what we find on each other, but, instead, we pay money to sit in a hot room, bathe in communal tubs, and have strangers rub our backs with scented oils. Often this kind of treatment costs a pretty penny—wouldn't you charge a lot to rub down a stranger?—and so the pampered expect a certain level of service. When the experience doesn't live up to the expectation, White Whines abound.

If you're a masseuse, pay special attention to this paragraph. Apparently, people hate it when you (1) talk to them during a massage, (2) massage too hard, and/or (3) massage too soft. There is a Goldilockian affliction among those on the table, where nothing the masseuse does seems to be just right. However frustrating it is to hear someone complain about the experience of being rubbed down with warm oil, it can be slightly offset by the thought that they might be leaving more stressed than when they came in.

The other thing people seem to really hate about the spa is that other people are there. Other people, as we all know, are uncultured barbarians and, therefore, should not be in the same pool as someone more deserving of the spa's many wonders. But there they are, pumicing their skin, talking on the phone, and doing any number of other uncouth things.

Perhaps the whiniest of all though are the people who never make it to the spa. Why? Because it's just a whole big thing, ya know? What with the driving, the robe, the endless massage, the countless oils, all the different pools and saunas to sit in, blah blah blah. It's just too much work for some people. Is that not among the ultimate White Whines? "This spa is too stressful" is up there with "This private jet is too loud" and "This lobster is too big" on the Things I Hope To Complain About One Day list.

Kari
White Whine

Dear masseuse lady I had today, please don't try to set me up with your nephew when you are rubbing my bare back #iwantedtorelax #smh 😫

3/2/13, 10:48 PM

58m

This morning I got a massage &the masseuse hummed for the entire hour.She also played 'this little pig went to...'with my toes. Most strange

Expand ← Reply ⇄ Retweet ★ Favorite

White Whine

To the woman in the spa: I know jacuzzis are teeming with bacteria but must you exfoliate your entire body with a pumice stone when there are other people sitting in it?!

Like · Comment · 10 hours ago via Mobile · ✿

White Whine

Tan-Trums

If there's anything worse than skin cancer, it's being pale. I know this because I am pale. In the right light, at the height of winter, I could blind an Inuit if I took my shirt off. The reason I don't tan, though, is because my family has a long, proud history of becoming covered with a malignant film of freckles if we spend too much time in the sun. But tanning fascinates me, not only because it produces freakish looking enthusiasts but also because people who tan regularly seem to really not like it all that much.

I'm talking, of course, about uneven tans. Or body parts getting tan that aren't supposed to get tan. Or getting too tan or not tan enough. Or the tanning bed being too cold or cramped. These are real concerns that White Whiney tanners have as they snap themselves into a coffin full of cancer-giving light.

I think what I love so much about people who complain about tanning is that it really highlights how far we've come as an animal. Here we've been able to harness the power of the sun, a ball of flame and fire so mighty that it warms us and burns us from almost a hundred million miles away. And once we were finally able to harness the power, we used it to make little boxes where orange people can bitch about how annoying it is when the magical bed with the power of the sun gets your lip all brown.

Good for us.

OH MY GOSH!!!! A mouse! a mouse! a mouse! Eeewwwwwww. In the garage and it's sleeting outside so I don't Blame him, but I want to tan and relax and now I'm just freaking out!!!!!! Eeeewwwwwww. Whine whine whine.

Like · Comment · 2 hours ago near ▬▬▬▬

👍 ▬▬▬▬ likes this.

▬▬▬▬ That sucks! Especially if u tan out there!
2 hours ago · Like

▬▬▬▬ um, kill it. Either that or realize that it wont hurt you.
2 hours ago · Like

▬▬▬▬ It does suck! My tanning bed is in a workshop area inside our garage so I know there can be spiders and flies and such. But never seen a mouse. :/
2 hours ago · Like

▬▬▬▬ Yeah. Thanks ▬▬▬. It ran away. I know it won't hurt me. Just gross.
2 hours ago · Like

▬▬▬▬ says "suck it up. this too shall pass"
2 hours ago · Like

White Whine

▬▬▬▬
My upper lip got tanned at the pool the other day. wtf. My life is over.

White Whine

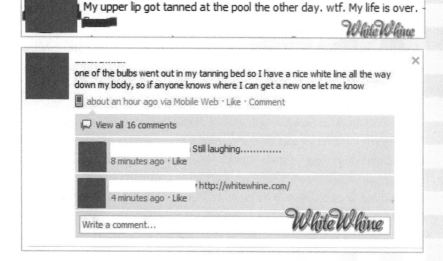

▬▬▬▬   ×
one of the bulbs went out in my tanning bed so I have a nice white line all the way down my body, so if anyone knows where I can get a new one let me know

about an hour ago via Mobile Web · Like · Comment

💬 View all 16 comments

▬▬▬▬ Still laughing.............
8 minutes ago · Like

▬▬▬▬ http://whitewhine.com/
4 minutes ago · Like

Write a comment...

White Whine

Tiffany?
You're Kidding Me

Most men have been lead to believe that Tiffany jewelry is the only thing women actually want. The myth states that the instant a woman sees the robin's egg blue box, her ovaries release dozens of eggs because she senses that a man worth breeding with is within sex distance. For the most part this seems to be true. I once had the horrible misfortune of watching my mother open a Tiffany box from my father, and then make unspeakable faces at him. Horrible, traumatizing faces that haunt me to this day . . .

Sorry, I need a moment.

Okay, where were we? Oh yes, Tiffany. While most women seem to truly love getting a little something from Tiffany, not all are so easy to please. There is a small group of White Whiners out there who absolutely despise Tiffany jewelry and, lucky for us, they go online and let the world know.

What makes Tiffany White Whiners stand out to me is that the jewelry is almost always given as a substitute for words that the men in their lives have trouble saying. Simple phrases like, "Darling, I love you," "Baby, you're my everything," and "Please honey, let me move back in! I'll never cheat on you again!" In other words, a gift from Tiffany carries more emotion than a nice sweater or a really nice digital picture frame. Because of that, we know that behind every one of these Tiffany White Whines, there's a guy feeling really, really upset that his love not only didn't appreciate the gesture but also decided to go online and let everyone else know how much she hated the charm bracelet.

Seriously. I asked for the iPhone 5. Not two stupid Tiffanys's & co. charm bracelets. What a shitty Christmas this is going to be. #sad

1:11pm - 11 Dec 12 from Durham, Ontario

I was really excited when I thought I got the cartier love bracelet for christmas & then I wasnt so excited when I saw it was tiffanys

12/26/12, 5:59 PM

White Whine

Like Visa, I'm Accepted Everywhere

I remember very vividly the day that I got accepted into college. My mother yelled upstairs to me one Saturday morning to say that a thick envelope had arrived from UConn. I quickly ran downstairs, tore open the envelope, saw the words "happy to inform you," and decided then and there that I wasn't going to give one more single shit about high school. I didn't really want to go to UConn, but it just felt good knowing that someone, somewhere thought I was good enough.

Now try to put yourself into the shoes of someone who hasn't received that big envelope yet. They've sent out dozens of applications but have yet to get a single "happy to inform you" back. Imagine the intense pressure of not knowing what the immediate future holds. Imagine waking up each morning, running to the mailbox, and finding no evidence that one single institute of higher learning thinks you're worthy yet. Imagine the sinking feeling that you, somehow, have been one of the unfortunates, doomed to stand on the dock of life and watch your friends sail off to sunnier shores while you load their bags. Imagine all of that and then imagine reading this White Whine.

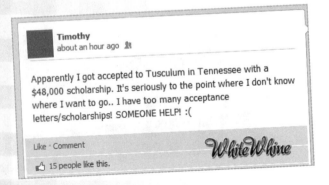

Timothy
about an hour ago

Apparently I got accepted to Tusculum in Tennessee with a $48,000 scholarship. It's seriously to the point where I don't know where I want to go.. I have too many acceptance letters/scholarships! SOMEONE HELP! :(

Like · Comment

White Whine

👍 15 people like this.

The *Doorman*

When you're a busy urban professional, you often don't have time to do things like carry your own groceries up to your apartment, check your own mail, or sign for your own packages. That's why a lot of city dwellers choose to live in buildings that come with their own slave, a doorman. A doorman works at the front desk, and his main job is getting yelled at by annoyed residents while opening the door. There are many benefits to having a doorman—such as having the door opened for you, and having someone to yell at. But not everybody is sold. One White Whiner in particular decided to create a doorman pro/con list in his head after living with one for two years.

He then inexplicably put that pro/con list on Facebook, presumably because he lost a bet or something.

2 years in and I'm still not quite sure my overall opinion on living in a doorman building, particularly vis-à-vis the type of place I'll ultimately buy in Manhattan. It's so damned convenient and pampering; on the other hand, a large part of me is too much of a privacy nut to ever truly be comfortable with some old white man knowing every package/meal that I have delivered and guest I have over.

Like · Comment · 37 minutes ago near New York · 🏢 *White Whine*

No Free Rides on the *Scholarship*

College is undeniably expensive, a fact that my parents have never failed to remind me of the past decade. If the current trajectory for college tuition is extrapolated and applied to the next fifty years, by 2063 the cost of going to a private four year college should be somewhere in the neighborhood of $12 million. Not surprisingly, many students choose to apply for scholarships, which are monetary gifts bestowed on students who are exceptionally smart, exceptionally dumb, or meet some qualification set forth by the institution granting the scholarship (for instance, the most accomplished eighteen-year-old balloon animal maker who is also deaf). It's that last one that really seems to irk white, middle-class students of average academic achievement.

Every scholarship season, thousands of oppressed white kids take to the Internet to declare it "soooooo unfair" that there aren't more academic opportunities for them (you know, besides all of the academic opportunities). They earnestly wish, if only for a few weeks, to have been born black, Asian, Hispanic, gay, crippled, blind, or otherwise "different" so they wouldn't be discriminated against. They point out that they did not choose to be born with white skin and into a comfortable home, so why should they be punished for it? It's a fair point, if a ridiculous one, because, after all, if they were allowed to choose, they'd probably want to be born white and comfortable anyway. Comfortable white people have it pretty good here.

It's easy to feel a creeping rage well up inside when indignant white kids complain about the lack of opportunities in this country. But let's remember that these kids are striving for an education, not a country club membership. However terrible one of them may seem at first read, always remind yourself that this kid, however pampered, however ridiculous, however ludicrously entitled he may be, just wants the opportunity to get a college degree.

For free.

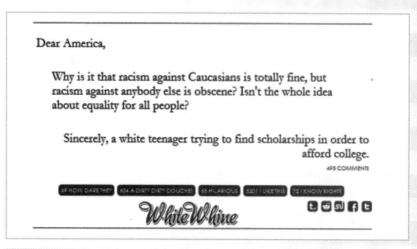

No Place Like *Home*

Most every first year college student is familiar with homesickness. I recall seeing more than a few people sitting in the dorm hallway, crying on the phone as they confessed to mom or dad that maybe this school just isn't right for them. I was definitely not one of those people, no matter what my hallmates might say after they read this part of the book. They're all liars, and not one of them should be trusted.

Anyway, it's understandable that a kid from a comfortable home would meet college with a mixture of fear, shock, and disgust. A new college student is basically a prisoner in the world's cushiest jail. He is forced to use a communal bathroom, told when to eat, and forced to live in a cinderblock box with a stranger who is almost definitely going to masturbate in front of him. In short, it's an adjustment.

Most kids make that adjustment fairly easily once they discover the perks of going to college: delayed adult responsibilities, plenty of co-ed sex to be had, unlimited fattening food, free-flowing alcohol, freely available drugs, and, of course, a wealth of knowledge to be gleaned from a learned body of professors (one of whom will probably sell you weed if you let him know you party).

Some kids, though, just can't wrap their heads around the fact that their college will not be quite as comfortable as the cushy home they just left behind. The fact that college is a privilege, often a very expensive one, doesn't cross their minds as they moan about the Internet speed, the dining hall food, and/or the lack of premium cable channels. They'll give school the old college try, but they're really going to need their college to try harder.

and not a single place on campus carries coconut water. what the fuck this isnt the 1800's like how could u not have coconut water

Expand

'@r 4h

sure u can buy groceries on campus but mcmaster's idea of groceries is fucking kraft dinner and goldfish crackers

Expand

r @r 4h

i want to buy groceries to take back w me to hamilton but i cant bring myself to do it bc i have a $3k meal plan i somehow need to use up

Expand

Corrin

what kind of a college doesn't take visa?!

5 hours ago · Like · Comment

Brady

Yesterday near New Haven, CT via mobile 🞓

Two Yale Dining grievances tonight:

1. Please don't serve me anything where the first ingredient is "pork butt." Even "pork posterior" would be kinder.

2. Just calling your tabbouleh "Mexican tabbouleh" does not make it a Mexican food...

Like · Comment

👍 9 people like this.

217

Hey UM Housing & Residential Life, why do we get HBO but it's not in HD? :(

Like · Comment · a few seconds ago · 👥   *White Whine*

---

via **Social Primer**
Washington University is left out again...

Brooks Brothers to Sell Harvard, Princeton, Cornell Licensed Apparel
racked.com

Brooks Brothers, the bastion of all things preppy, has announced that this August, it will release a line of licensed collegiate apparel bearing the school colors and insignias of...

↩ 10 hours ago · Like · Comment · Share   *White Whine*

I hate maids on campus. I was trying to sleep this morning. She knocked like 20 times, and then tried all the keys making as much noise as possible before she even got in the room, then she turned on all the lights, vacuumed right next to my face, and finally she left and left all the lights on. -_-

Like · Comment · 33 minutes ago near Orlando, FL · ✳

👍 Tae Nicholas likes this.

what a bitch
30 minutes ago · Like

z hahah getting your moneys worth
29 minutes ago · Like

I know that feel.
http://www.tinygif.net/pictures/12606938664f068bf2ef87f.gif
29 minutes ago · Like · 👍 1

ike xD
27 minutes ago · Like · 👍 1   *White Whine*

@nick accurate.....
26 minutes ago · Like

#CollegePeopleProblems
25 minutes ago · Like

LITERALLY say the same thing every thursday.
17 minutes ago · Like

Next time rise out of bed like some crazy zombie and attack her, biting her wherever possible. You can blame it on being woken so suddenly and she'll never be back.
14 minutes ago · Like

$Luxury^2$

I've spent this entire book making fun of White Whiners and their major complaints about minor inconveniences in their otherwise wonderful lives. But the truth is if you're living in the developed world, you're almost certainly guilty of White Whining yourself. I suffer frequent First-World Problems, and no matter how much I try to hold my tongue, I always manage to let a few slip. My dog walker doesn't put the coat on my dog in the winter. My parents' pool was too cold to swim in. My wife got me the last generation iPad for my birthday instead of the new one. Even this book—something I've wanted to do for seven years—was initially met with a torrent of complaints about how long contracts take to finalize and, later, pitiful moans about how hard it is to write a book.

But I'm not rich—shocking, I know—and that sad fact prevents me from becoming a truly great White Whiner. You see, most First-World Problems usually contain only one reference to something that could be called luxurious. "I had a middle seat on the flight all the way to Bermuda." "Ugh, I ate too much lobster." "I lost my Amex Platinum!" These are all White Whines that could reasonably be said by a normal, middle-class person. The truly spoiled can take it further.

Bird
10 hours ago near Fort Wayne via mobile

Gonna get ready for my first class. I'd rather just lay under my SUV and let the nanny run me over. Ugh.

Like · Comment · Share

2 people like this.

White Whine

"When I fly private to Bermuda, I shouldn't have to put my phone on airplane mode." "My personal chef made wayyy too much lobster." "Anyone in Monaco find an Amex black card with my name on it? Lost it at the bar last night." Can you spot the difference? There's a primary luxury—going to Bermuda, eating lobster, having an Amex black card—but there's also a kicker luxury—private jet, personal chef, being in Monaco. Often the secondary luxury is an afterthought, not really being the subject of the whine but rather a detail slipped in to further paint the tragic scene. With this method, the level of White Whininess—and the degree of "oh shut the fuck up"-ness you'll feel upon hearing it—is compounded.

It doesn't have to stop at two luxuries, either. I've never seen it, but theoretically a White Whine could exist with up to ten referenced luxuries. Here is an example: "My girlfriend and I were back from a modeling shoot in St. Croix and were playing golf with my new Callaways in the Hamptons near my family's summer house with some friends from Harvard. My driver (car, not club) was over by one of the Bentleys when I hooked a drive and hit him in the throat, killing him instantly (Callaways are fast clubs). Father's attorneys $moothed it over with the guy's widow and children for me, but still, annoying, right?"

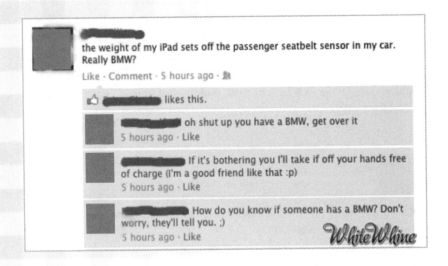

the weight of my iPad sets off the passenger seatbelt sensor in my car. Really BMW?

Like · Comment · 5 hours ago ·

👍 ⬛⬛⬛ likes this.

⬛⬛⬛ oh shut up you have a BMW, get over it
5 hours ago · Like

⬛⬛⬛ If it's bothering you I'll take if off your hands free of charge (I'm a good friend like that :p)
5 hours ago · Like

⬛⬛⬛ How do you know if someone has a BMW? Don't worry, they'll tell you. ;)
5 hours ago · Like

White Whine

3 hours ago near Toronto 🙎

Time for the whitest of white whines:

That delicious lobster feast ruined my manicure.

Like · Comment

 and 2 others like this. *WhiteWhine*

Monday near Bluffton, SC 🙎

I love my housekeeper... but her assistant is an absolute ass, poor Debbie had to go behind her and redo constantly .... so I told her not to bring her back to my house in the future.

Like · Comment *WhiteWhine*

 That's not cool... I'd have done the same.
Monday at 9:11am · Like

 In a time when people actually want and need jobs you would think she would put a little more effort into her work and god almighty was she rude to Debbie... grrrr.
Monday at 9:14am · Like · 👍 1

 Yep, you would think...
Monday at 10:03am · Like

 I've had a few maids who really let the ball drop. Thats why I don't have one anymore. Its too much trouble to pick up for the maid and then wonder what they are doing.
Monday at 2:03pm · Like

 M

would be watching true blood but there's no HBO at my beach house :(
10 hours ago · Like · Comment *WhiteWhine*

Conclusion

Well that's it, I'm afraid. I hope you've enjoyed the book so much that you refuse to lend it to anyone and insist they buy their own copy. And as much fun as it is to laugh at all of these White Whiners, I think this whole book points to a larger truth about mankind: We are an unsatisfied species. No amount of pampering or luxury can change that. We're always peeking into the neighbors' yard to see what they have, even when to do so requires climbing on top of our family estate's perimeter wall. We are constantly striving for better circumstances: We lived in caves, we wanted houses; we rode horses, we wanted cars; we gathered food and hunted animals, we wanted to farm and raise livestock. Our ceaseless drive for circumstantial improvement is the reason we built cities; the reason we created universities; the reason we wrote books; the reason we invented medicine; the reason we care for our elderly and our infants; the reason we unlocked the mysteries of the universe, large and small, forging us into the only beings, thus far, capable of seeing ourselves, our world, and all that ever was and ever will be in the greater context of time and space.

It's also the reason we called the Starbucks barista a retard on Twitter when she gave us skim instead of soy.

Thanks for reading. Please visit WhiteWhine.com for more hilarious First-World Problems.

About the Author

Streeter Seidell is the creator of WhiteWhine.com and editor-in-chief of CollegeHumor.com. He lives in Brooklyn with his endlessly patient wife.